A GREEN INDUSTRIAL POLICY FOR EUROPE

Simone Tagliapietra and Reinhilde Veugelers

BRUEGEL BLUEPRINT SERIES
A green industrial policy for Europe

Simone Tagliapietra and Reinhilde Veugelers

Editor: Stephen Gardner
Layout and cover design: Hèctor Badenes

© Bruegel 2020 All rights reserved. Short sections of text, not to exceed two paragraphs, may be quoted in the original language without explicit permission provided that the source is acknowledged. Opinions expressed in this publications are those of the author alone.

Bruegel
33, rue de la Charité, Box 4
1210 Brussels, Belgium
www.bruegel.org

ISBN: 978-9-078910-50-3

Acknowledgements

The authors are grateful to André Sapir, Guntram Wolff and Maria Demertzis for their extensive comments on preliminary drafts. They would like to thank Enrico Bergamini for his excellent contribution in drafting the literature review underpinning chapters 1, 2 and 3 and the case studies in chapter 6. Tom Schraepen and Ben McWilliams provided excellent research assistance.

This Blueprint has been produced with the financial support of the European Climate Foundation.

Contents

About the authors 3
Foreword 5
Executive summary 6

1 Defining green industrial policy 12

2 The history of industrial policy in Europe 17

3 Classic arguments for industrial policy 23

4 New industrial policy 27

5 A new green industrial policy 37
    5.1 A bold green industrial policy: urgency, risk-taking,
    experimentation 37
    5.2 A balanced mix of green industrial policy instruments 40
    5.3 A global green industrial policy: avoiding the tragedy of the
    commons 41
    5.4 Addressing green industrial policy government failures 42
    5.5 Summary: lessons for green industrial policy 44

6 Green industrial policy in practice 47
    6.1 Germany 47
    6.2 Netherlands 51
    6.3 Denmark 53

    6.4 United States 55
    6.5 Lessons learned 56

7   Green industrial policy in the EU 58
    7.1 The status of green industrial policy in the EU 58
    7.2 The European Commission's 'New industrial strategy for Europe'
    and its green aspect 61
    7.3 The EU's main green industrial policy tools 63

8   Conclusions and policy recommendations 79
    8.1 Strong governance 79
    8.2 Tackling geographical fragmentation 81
    8.3 Managing long-term expectations with a solid EU
    decarbonisation trajectory 82
    8.4 Development of sound public-private partnerships 83
    8.5 Stimulating EU green investment 85
    8.6 Stimulating EU green science and innovation 86
    8.7 A global approach 87
    8.8 Communicate transparently 88

References 89

About the authors

Simone Tagliapietra is a Research Fellow at Bruegel and an adjunct professor at the Università Cattolica del Sacro Cuore and at the Johns Hopkins University School of Advanced International Studies. His research focuses on European Union climate and energy policy, the political economy of EU decarbonisation, green industrial policy, just transition and global climate governance. He is the author of *Global energy fundamentals* (Cambridge University Press, 2020) and *L'energia del mondo* (Il Mulino, 2020).

Reinhilde Veugelers is a Senior Fellow at Bruegel and a professor at KULeuven (Belgium). She is also a Centre for Economic Policy Research Fellow, a non-resident Senior Fellow at the Peterson Institute for International Economics and a member of the Royal Flemish Academy of Belgium for Sciences and of the Academia Europeana. She was previously an advisor in the European Commission's Bureau of European Policy Analysis and a member of the European Research Council Scientific Council. Her research concentrates on industrial organisation, international economics and strategy, and innovation and science. She is a member of the Board of Reviewing Editors of the journal *Science*.

Foreword

The European Green Deal, the flagship initiative of the European Commission under Ursula von der Leyen, aims at making Europe climate-neutral by 2050. The European Council has decided on the goal of reducing the European Union's emissions by 55 percent relative to their 1990 level by 2030. These are ambitious goals and putting them into practice will be extremely challenging from political, distributional and technological perspectives. We are only at the beginning of a major endeavour. Europe cannot afford to fail.

To succeed, decarbonisation has to accelerate in all industries and sectors across Europe. The European Green Deal must foster major shifts from fossil fuels to renewables. For example, the internal combustion engine in vehicles will need to be replaced by electricity or hydrogen. Industrial processes will need to reduce their dependence on coal and oil. Green energy production capacities must be increased.

Shifting the economy from brown to green represents one of the biggest socio-economic transformations ever seen in history. Not by coincidence, this challenge is often referred to as an industrial revolution against a deadline. Without significant technological advancements, the industrial revolution will become too expensive to be socially acceptable. And relying only on price signals may mean that technological change happens to late. Green industrial policy therefore needs to be a cornerstone of the European Green Deal.

But what is green industrial policy? What makes it different from general industrial policy? What are the market failures it should address? What are the main principles it should respond to and its main policy instruments? How can the mistakes of previous industrial policies be avoided? Will states be ready to accept risks when trying to foster breakthrough technologies? What governance mechanisms should be established to ensure countries end support when projects are failing?

In the EU context, an important factor is the interplay between green industrial policy and the single market. Industrial policy is national and is closely monitored by the EU's state aid and competition policy watchdog. But green industrial policy may be more acceptable given the public-policy need to accelerate innovation to achieve climate targets. But as this happens, the risk of fragmentation of Europe's single market will increase. A major theme of Europe's green industrial policy is therefore how it can ensure a level playing field.

So far, the EU has failed to provide the coherent green industrial policy framework that is required to turn the European Green Deal into an industrial opportunity for Europe. I sincerely hope this Blueprint will spark a fresh discussion on the principles and policy tools that should underpin Europe's green industrial policy. I would like to thank the authors for their work and the European Climate Foundation for their financial support for this work.

Guntram Wolff, Director of Bruegel
Brussels, December 2020

Executive summary

The European Green Deal aims to make Europe the first climate-neutral continent by 2050. This is not going to be an easy journey. To be successful, the European Green Deal will have to foster major shifts in the European industrial structure, including transitions from fossil fuels to renewable energy and from combustion engine cars to electric cars. Shifting economies from brown to green would be a major, historic socio-economic transformation. Not by coincidence, this challenge is often referred to as an industrial revolution against a deadline. In this context of broad, paradigmatic, change for European industry, a 'green industrial policy' will be fundamental to Europe's climate change ambitions.

In March 2020, the European Commission published a *New Industrial Strategy for Europe* (COM (2020) 102 final). Despite its focus on the twin green and digital transitions, the strategy failed to provide the coherent European Union green industrial policy framework that is required to turn the green transition into an industrial opportunity for Europe. In her September 2020 State of the Union speech, Commission President Ursula von der Leyen pledged to update the industrial strategy in the first half of 2021. This Blueprint aims to contribute to this debate, by setting out a set of principles and guidelines for the development of a strong EU green industrial policy.

These principle and guidelines have been developed on the basis of an in-depth analysis of the existing literature on industrial policy design and selected case studies. There are limits to what the market and the state can each deliver. For a successful green industrial policy, mechanisms will be needed to make them work together efficiently.

The design of public-private partnerships will make or break green industrial policy efforts. The major transformative change demanded by climate change will also require the involvement of civil society more than in other areas of industrial policy. Green technologies, often still emerging, are complex and uncertain. Future uncertainty about climate and technology scenarios underlines the importance of industry-research collaboration.

This Blueprint is structured as follows:

- Chapter 1 introduces the concept of green industrial policy, distinguishing it from general industrial policy, and from climate policy.
- Chapter 2 then discusses the practice of industrial policy in Europe, from the protectionism of the early twentieth century to the current industrial policy revival because of both the climate crisis and COVID-19.
- Chapter 3 sets out the theory of industrial policy and the academic debate between state interventionists and free-marketers. Particular attention is devoted to the notions of market and government failures as a framework for discussing industrial policy.
- Chapter 4 describes the most recent developments in the academic debate on industrial policy, seeking to reconcile the two traditional schools of thought. It introduces a new perspective for industrial policy that takes a broader approach and focuses not only on policy tools, but also on the policy process, most notably the involvement and coordination of, and the sharing of information between, the government, private sector and civil society.
- Chapter 5 discusses the characteristics of green industrial policy, in the context of the urgency of the climate crisis, the broad spectrum of green transition challenges and the nature of the specific market and government failures that characterise green technologies.
- Switching from theory to practice, chapter 6 discusses green industrial policy in Germany, the Netherlands, Denmark and the United States. From these case studies, we extrapolate a set of lessons,

including the importance of effective collaboration between all parts of society, the importance of policy stability and long-term predictability, and the development of balanced sets of instruments that mix demand pull and technology push.
- Chapter 7 gives an overview of Europe's green industrial policy landscape. It focuses in particular on the wide variety of tools available at EU level, from competition policy to innovation policy, and from development policy to climate policy.

Based on this analysis, our main recommendations for the development of an EU green industrial policy are:

Green industrial policy cannot be only national: EU-wide coordination is required

Europe is characterised by a multitude of green industrial policy initiatives, undertaken at regional, national and EU levels. These initiatives are generally not coordinated, and may even conflict. This is a major issue, because significantly different green industrial policies in different EU countries fragment the EU single market and could disrupt the level playing field. A fragmented EU single market for green technologies prevents innovative European cleantech companies from scaling up in the way that their United States and Chinese competitors do on their domestic markets. It is thus vital to develop a solid regulatory framework accompanied by competition policy enforcement, ensuring access to a truly single, competitive EU market with common environmental standards. In other words, the EU single market is a key asset for the development of an EU green industrial policy. Furthermore, European countries and companies would benefit greatly from joint coordinated actions in certain green technologies, so that they can internalise externalities and exploit synergies and economies of scale. Such coordinated actions should learn from past failures, such as Germany's unsuccessful attempts at developing a solar panel industry despite generous solar energy subsidies.

Strong governance will be essential

To develop a successful green industrial policy, the EU must work closely with the private sector. Public-private partnerships are not only about co-financing of initiatives, but are also about ensuring access to skills, knowledge and information. But close public-private interaction involves risks, such as rent-seeking and political capture. To address risks, a clear set of targets and milestones and well-structured procedures of accountability and transparency are needed.

European Alliances should be further expanded

European Alliances – already established since 2017 for batteries and since 2020 for clean hydrogen – foster public-private collaboration and should be expanded, making them deeper and broader. First, these Alliances should focus on addressing mega-problems covering the whole value chain, and not only manufacturing. This is relevant where most of the economic growth and job-creation potential in a value chain lies in installation and maintenance, rather than in the manufacturing – as is the case for solar energy or residential energy efficiency, for example. Second, these Alliances should involve emerging and innovative industrial and other stakeholders alongside established industrial players. Third, state aid rules should be revisited to check whether they are suitable for broadening and deepening of Important Projects of Common European Interest, which are at the core of these Alliances.

The EU should be braver in fostering green disruptive innovation

Green industrial policy needs breakthrough innovation. This requires significant risk-taking by public institutions, and an acceptance that there will be failures. New support models that provide numerous but still-sizeable grants via relatively non-bureaucratic channels are crucial to stimulate frontier ideas. Policy should not lead to money being put only on safe bets that offer average returns. In this sense, the innovation component of EU green industrial policy should be viewed as a portfolio, in which certain initiatives will inevitably fail. A portfolio with no failures entails no risks, and a portfolio with no risks is unlikely to provide breakthrough innovation. More new policy initiatives designed and monitored as experiments should be tried.

EU investment is important for financing green industrial policy initiatives
EU green investment will play an important role in realising the green transition, including by mobilising funds from national budgets and the private sector. The decision to devote 30 percent of the EU 2021-2027 budget and 37 percent of Next Generation EU funding to climate action is good news. However, the European Commission should develop a solid methodology for monitoring climate spending to avoid risks of greenwashing. The European Investment Bank (EIB) should be allowed to truly become Europe's climate bank, notably via a capital increase that will increase its firepower. The EIB should also further develop its role as financier of the green transition, including by playing the important role of connecting, as an intermediary, the relevant public and private stakeholders and supporting their interactions.

Finally, the EU should seize the current opportunity to become a global standard-setter for green bonds, given that it is the biggest player on this rapidly growing market.

EU green industrial policy should go beyond Europe's borders
Europe produces less than 10 percent of global greenhouse gas emissions. To really make a difference in terms of climate protection, the European Green Deal has to go beyond Europe's borders. It is of paramount importance for Europe to fill the current global leadership vacuum in climate terms, and to initiate and build global partnerships with other countries. In its relations with developing countries, we recommend that the EU should focus its external development policy more on supporting green projects financially and with capacity-building activities. Such an approach would provide a triple benefit. First,

it would help meet the EU's climate finance obligations and thus help to achieve the conditional emission-reduction commitments made by most developing countries under the Paris Agreement. Second, it would help EU industry to enter into new, rapidly growing markets. And third, it would help economic development in the EU's partner countries, providing an invaluable foreign policy dividend for the EU.

1 Defining green industrial policy

In December 2019, the then-newly appointed President of the European Commission, Ursula von der Leyen, published amid great fanfare a proposal for a European Green Deal, which has the fundamental aim of making Europe the first climate-neutral continent by 2050. In September 2020, it was followed up with a proposal to achieve net-zero emissions, centred on the acceleration of the European Union decarbonisation process over the next ten years, with a steeper EU emissions reduction target for 2030 of at least 55 percent relative to 1990 (compared to a 40% reduction target currently). The plan also addresses the economic and industrial transformation this necessarily implies, and aims to make the overall process socially inclusive.

It will not be an easy ride. A successful European Green Deal will have to foster major shifts in the European economic structure, including transitions from fossil fuels to renewable energy and from diesel to electric cars. This will be a broad, paradigmatic, change to our economies and a historic major socio-economic transformation. For good reason, this challenge is often referred to as an industrial revolution against a deadline.

As in any major transformation, there will be winners and losers, particularly in the short-run. With the European Green Deal, the EU recognises that climate and energy policies alone are not sufficient to pursue climate neutrality. For instance, a strategy only based on raising the price of carbon would not deliver on the goals if people will fiercely reject it – as seen in France with the *gilets jaunes* movement. Only a much broader policy – also encompassing economic, industrial, fiscal, labour, innovation and social policy aspects – can meet such a vast challenge, creating more winners than losers. The European Green Deal seeks to facilitate this challenging broader process by providing a clear sense of direction to investors and citizens and by putting in place mechanisms to ensure that the most vulnerable segments of society are supported and not left behind.

It is often said that the European Green Deal must turn decarbonisation into an opportunity to revitalise the European economy, and thus to ensure long-term economic growth and jobs. That is, while heading towards climate neutrality by 2050, the European economy has to remain highly competitive at global level, in the context of increasing competition from other major economies. This puts green industrial policy in the spotlight, in the context of a debate about it that has gathered fresh momentum in recent years (see Lane, 2019; Rodrik, 2014; Rodrik and Sabel, 2019; Aiginer and Rodrik, 2020; and Cherif and Hasanov, 2019, among many others).

A first challenge when entering into this debate is to define what green industrial policy is about. It is already a challenge to define industrial policy. Any government policy will have some impact on the economic structure of a country. To narrow down the focus of the analysis, it is useful to start by discussing the objectives of industrial policy [1].

In the established literature, a common factor in all definitions of industrial policy is that it targets a set of economic activities to achieve long-term benefits for society. New tendencies in the industrial policy literature, which we label 'new industrial policy' (NIP), stress that industrial policy should have aims beyond short-term competitiveness and economic growth. It should have a broader multi-dimensional

---

1 This is also how, for instance, Ambroziak (2017) approached the issue, in a literature review covering more than 110 publications. The falling share of manufacturing and the digitalisation of the economy, among other factors, are changing the nature of industry itself. Ambroziak (2017) concluded that the definition of industrial policy is subject to the same transformation the definition of 'industry' itself faces.

objective, which can be captured in the notion of long-term social welfare. This is the case, for instance, in Rodrik and Sabel (2019), who set out to rethink and investigate *"a set of interventions"* which should have as their goal a *"good jobs economy"*.

Delineation of a 'green' version of industrial policy becomes necessary once decarbonisation is set as a societal goal, as Europe has done with the European Green Deal. While the goal of climate policy is decarbonisation and the goal of (new) industrial policy is social welfare, green industrial policy must reconcile the goals of decarbonising the economy (like climate policy) and social welfare (like industrial policy) (Figure 1). We can thus define green industrial policy as an industrial policy in which climate change mitigation becomes a binding constraint in achieving the social welfare goal.

Figure 1: Green industrial policy

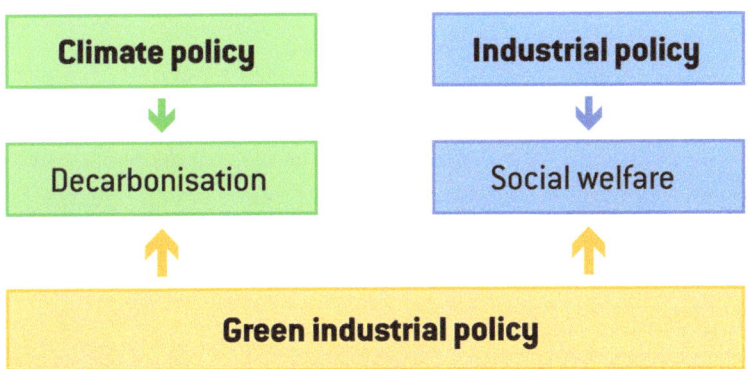

Source: Bruegel.

This combination of objectives immediately identifies the challenge of green industrial policy, which is to meet both goals simultaneously. This becomes particularly challenging when they conflict, when trade-offs have to be decided on, and when costs must be attached when one of the goals is not being met.

Furthermore, green industrial policy will operate alongside climate policy and industrial policy more generally and therefore raises the issue of coordination of the various policies, particularly when they are overseen by different institutions or departments. Climate policy and industrial policy each have their own instruments. Is coordination of the already existing climate change and industrial policy instruments sufficient to establish a green industrial policy? Does green industrial policy need its own policy instruments? If so, how should they be coordinated with existing instruments?

Green industrial policy, like any policy, is a public intervention aimed at correcting problems. Industrial policy addresses problems including financial market imperfections that lead to constraints on access to finance, research externalities[2] that cause constraints on access to knowledge, labour market imperfections that limit access to skills and network externalities that hinder partnerships[3]. These constraints may lead to markets failing to grow, while preventing new markets from emerging and developing.

In addition to tackling market failures, which is the core of classic industrial policy, green industrial policy must also address market failures associated with climate change. The main market failure in climate terms is that greenhouse gas emissions are a side-effect of economically valuable activities, but those responsible for the emissions do not pay the costs. The adverse effects of greenhouse gases are therefore 'external' to the market, which means there is usually only an

---

2 Research and development (R&D) activities are widely considered to have positive effects beyond those enjoyed by the funders of R&D (normally, the companies that pay for the research). This is because R&D adds to the general body of knowledge, contributing to other discoveries and developments. However, the returns to a firm selling products based on its own R&D typically do not include the returns to others who benefited indirectly.

3 Network externalities are the phenomenon by which the value or utility a user derives from a good or service depends on the number of users of compatible products. Network externalities are typically positive, resulting in a given user deriving more value from a product as other users join the same network.

ethical – rather than an economic – incentive for businesses and consumers to reduce their emissions. Consequently, the market fails by over-producing greenhouse gases. Economists have long argued that the first-best policy to correct this market failure is to apply a cost to greenhouse gas emissions in order to encourage reductions. Without a high enough carbon price, policymakers must fall back on second-best policy interventions, including regulation. Being generalised and technology-neutral, carbon pricing represents a superior policy tool, also because it avoids the risk that more targeted policies might bring of selecting wrongly (eg subsidising certain industries that ultimately go bankrupt).

The combination of classic market failure externalities and the greenhouse-gas externality represents a significant challenge for green industrial policy. It implies that green industrial policy requires the deployment of specific instruments that go beyond typical general industrial policy measures. These instruments do not need to be new instruments, but should at least be tailored to fit into a green industrial policy. A green industrial policy mix should in any case be developed in coordination with the policy instruments used for climate policy and industrial policy. Carbon pricing, for example, is an important part of the green industrial policy mix because if the price of carbon remains too low to drive low-carbon technology innovation in industry and other sectors of the economy, green industrial policy will have to fall-back on second-best options.

This Blueprint set out green industrial policy design guidelines, based on an in-depth review of the academic literature and a critical assessment of past policy experiences

.

2 The history of industrial policy in Europe

The industrial policy debate has historically been a debate on the role of the state in the economy: why, how and to what degree should governments intervene in steering markets? Should governments support 'winners'?

Before 1914, the main aim of industrial policy in Europe was to protect economies via tariffs (Foreman-Peck, 2006). Government intervention focused on the provision of infrastructure, favouring specific manufacturing businesses in which the state had an ownership and investment interest. Sectors targeted for intervention were largely natural monopolies, including railways and utilities. Tariffs on industrial and agricultural products were the main tools of industrial policy, with significant variation between, and competition among, countries. Less-developed countries had typically higher tariffs than advanced countries, which had more open economies. Another instrument was the protection of intellectual property, aimed at incentivising innovation. Countries that wanted to catch up technologically exploited the absence of intellectual property protection.

Between 1914 and 1950, European states intervened increasingly in economies devastated by war. The state played a major role in steering resources, not only under the dictatorships in Europe, but also in more traditionally liberal countries including France and Belgium. The 1929 crisis led to several industrial crises, which required state intervention. This was also legitimised in national debates by the successful experience of economic planning in the Soviet Union in terms of avoiding the deep economic downturn (Foreman-Peck, 2006). The role of the state in the economy thus emerged from war considerably strengthened in Europe. A prime example from this era was the creation of the *Istituto per la Ricostruzione Industriale* (IRI), an Italian public holding company established in 1933 by the fascist regime to rescue banks and private companies from bankruptcy during the Great Depression.

After the Second World War, the process of European reconstruction began, with a focus on strategic industries including coal, steel, electricity and railways. The period between the 1950s and the 1980s is referred to as the heyday of industrial policy, during which there was an increasing preoccupation to match United States levels of competitiveness (Owen, 2012). Industrial policy was extremely interventionist, as European governments ventured into picking winners through sectoral policies, also defined as vertical industrial policies. These policies were aimed at sectors thought to be strategic and promising for the future, including steel, chemicals, mechanics, communications and technology, aviation and nuclear power. Europe saw a wave of nationalisation and strong intervention via state-owned enterprises and other state-powered initiatives. It was in this period that the National Enterprise Board (1975) was set up in the United Kingdom to acquire a substantial level of equity in major manufacturing companies. France created the CNRS (*Centre national de la recherche scientifique*) and engaged in *'Grands Projets'*. West Germany followed a less-interventionist approach to catch up with the other economies on both sides of the Atlantic. These initiatives were mostly national. In this era, European institutions were still in their early development.

At the European level, the European Coal and Steel Community (ECSC) was set up in 1952 with the goal of reducing overcapacity in coal production, while improving the overall production system. This first industrial policy was considered a success in terms of both outcome (modernisation and reduction of production capacities of companies) and coordination between member states. The ECSC provided an interventionist framework within which companies had to modernise. The European Economic Community (EEC), established after the ECSC, progressively reduced tariffs in European markets. The first technology policy initiative at European Community level was PREST (*Politique de recherche scientifique et de technologie*), which sought to facilitate common European research projects. This initiative was underpinned by fears of European technology lagging behind American technology. In 1971, the European Cooperation in Science and Technology (COST) framework for intra-European research collaboration was established. In this phase, the development of a European industrial policy was hindered by the *"reluctance of governments, especially in the larger countries, to subordinate their national interests to those of Europe as a whole"* (Owen, 2012). A notable milestone in this era was the Colonna memorandum, which raised concerns about foreign direct investment from the United States going into high-technology industries in Europe. As a follow-up to the Colonna memorandum, and in reaction to a steel industry crisis, the European Commission adopted in 1977 the Davignon Plan, which aimed to stabilise the steel market by controlling prices and capacity, and also raised the prospect of *"European-wide solutions in the so-called 'sunset' industries and [...] keeping national control over 'sunrise' industries"* (Owen, 2012, p21), such as computers. It was in this context that the Airbus consortium was established, as a European industrial alliance for the production of aircraft.

The 1980s saw a new phase of liberalisation, championed by Margaret Thatcher and Ronald Reagan. During the so-called Washington Consensus, government intervention was deemed as detrimental for economic growth, inaugurating an era of market-oriented policies, during which a *laissez-faire* approach was taken to industrial policy, or, at most, industrial policy was limited to setting the right framework within which economic processes can take place (horizontal industrial policy). During this phase in Europe, the state became less interventionist. Countries liberalised markets, trying to avoid the failures of past industrial policy (typically vertical industrial policy and winner-picking). At European level, the inefficiency of uncoordinated national industrial policies became clear and led to the development of two important instruments at EU level: the internal market and competition policy, including state aid. The Single European Act (1986) also created the legal basis for affirmative action by the state in the area of research and development. During this time, different initiatives were undertaken at European Communities level to promote research and innovation cooperation. An example was ESPRIT (European Strategic Programme for Research and Information Technology), a five-year collaborative research programme with a goal of *"bringing together companies, universities and research institutes across Europe"* with a specific focus on information technology (Owen, 2012). ESPRIT was an attempt to respond to the government-led initiatives to bring together market and public participants undertaken by the Japanese Ministry for International Trade and Industry. These initiatives were effective in helping Japan quickly catch up with the United States as a technological and economic leader, particularly in the field of semiconductors. ESPRIT was the precursor of the Commission's Framework Programmes for R&D (starting in 1984), through which science, technology and innovation policy and collaborative research initiatives have been put in place, including Horizon 2020 (2014 to 2020) and the next version, Horizon Europe.

During the 1990s and early 2000s, liberalisation programmes continued in Europe. At EU level, a consensus was gradually built around a more holistic, integrated, horizontal approach to industrial policy, with EU industrial policy confined to a role of ensuring the right framework conditions, through the use of internal market and competition instruments and by stimulating R&D and innovation. This resulted in the Lisbon Strategy, a programme *"to transform the EU into the most competitive and dynamic knowledge-based economy in the world capable of sustainable economic growth with more and better jobs and greater social cohesion*"⁴. The strategy's aim was to implement a comprehensive set of structural reforms based on boosting innovation and investment in R&D, a more integrated and competitive internal market and a more flexible labour market.

The Great Recession in 2008 and its aftermath revived interest in industrial policy in Europe, as continuing economic crisis put manufacturing production and industrial jobs under pressure. In this environment, the European Commission published an updated plan for reindustrialising Europe, focusing on the need for a comprehensive vision for boosting the competitiveness of European companies. This was to involve all the levers available at EU level, including the single market, trade policy, policy towards small and medium enterprises, competition policy, environment policy and research policy.

Since then, a consensus has grown around a normalisation of industrial policy, acknowledging the need for government intervention, shifting the debate away from whether governments should do industrial policy at all to how they can do it well. The increasing pressure to decarbonise Europe and the world to address the global warming challenge has supported this resurgent stronger role of the state in Europe. The COVID-19 crisis has further reinforced the role of the state, which has had to intervene to combat the pandemic.

Figure 2: Timeline of European industrial policy

Pre-1914	1914-1950	1950-1980	1980s	1990-2000s	Recent years
Tariffs and protection of intellectual property	Growing state intervention	Winner-picking through vertical industrial policy	Market-oriented policies	Lisbon Agenda and further liberalisation	Renewed state interventionism, also due to the climate crisis and (more recently) COVID-19

Source: Bruegel.

4   See https://www.consilium.europa.eu/ueDocs/cms_Data/docs/pressData/en/ec/00100-r1.en0.htm.

The climate crisis together with COVID-19 have made clear that for resilient growth after the pandemic, not only will state intervention be needed, a different way of doing things will also be needed. Bowles and Carlin (2020) argued that: *"No combination of government fiat and market incentives, however cleverly designed, will produce solutions to problems like the pandemic,"* stressing the role of civil society in the gap between the state and the market. A very similar argument can be made for the climate crisis.

Future industrial policy also faces other challenges. Haskel and Westlake (2018) showed that the economy is becoming more *"intangible"*, meaning that businesses are increasingly investing in intangible assets, such as computerised information, knowledge, organisational processes, marketing, R&D, design and strong supply chains. They argued that this shift has major consequences for industrial policy, as intangible assets differ considerably from tangibles in four ways: they are more likely to be highly scalable, their costs are more likely to be sunk, they are more likely to have spillovers and they are more likely have synergies with each other. These characteristics create new market failures and shift the importance of others. Industrial policy should address these developments, most importantly because governments need to act to accommodate the necessary changes, including by providing public knowledge infrastructure and clarifying intellectual property regulation.

This makes it clear how challenging green industrial policy is. To be successful in the long term, it needs to reconcile policy and tools dealing with classic market-failure externalities and the greenhouse-gas externality, while taking into account a changing economy.

3 Classic arguments for industrial policy

At the core of the debate about industrial policy between state interventionists and free-marketers who oppose any form of market interference is the notion of market failures as justification for state intervention. Several market failures can provide a justification for correction via industrial policy: knowledge spill-overs, dynamic scale economies, coordination failures and informational externalities.

The early approach to industrial policy through trade protection was based on the infant-industry argument, an example of dynamic scale economies. Production costs may initially be higher for newly established domestic companies than for well-established foreign competitors, which have accumulated more experience. Over time, however, domestic producers can reduce costs as they learn by doing and/or achieve greater critical scale over time (dynamic scale economies). They may even overtake their foreign rivals if they can exploit some comparative advantage. Yet, if future returns outweigh initial losses, and it is only a matter of bridging, capital markets could finance the necessary investment needed by domestic companies (Baldwin, 1969). For the infant-industries argument for industrial policy to be justified, failings in the capital market are therefore also needed. Such capital market imperfections are likely to be present particularly in highly uncertain environments, and when firms and funders do not have equal access to information.

As intangible assets become more important, the infant-industry argument for industrial policy intervention becomes even more powerful. Compared to entrants, incumbent firms may be better able to exploit the synergies between new and existing intangible assets, giving them a major advantage over entrants, especially for more incremental innovative investments. The emerging role of big data in firms' business models illustrates this. Incumbents are able to expand their databases, run algorithms, draw conclusions and improve their services and operations, which in turn gives them access to more data. In comparison, an entrant with access to only a limited set of data cannot benefit from this positive feedback loop. In addition, an intangible economy makes life harder for infant firms, as they face tighter financial constraints. Intangible asset investments are most prone to capital market imperfections. They are not always visible on balance sheets and require investors to spend increasing amounts of time researching the firm (Haskel and Westlake, 2018). The infant-industry argument is therefore especially relevant in an intangible asset world, especially for newly emerging technologies and markets.

The perhaps most often used argument for industrial policy relates to R&D and technology policy and has to do with market failures arising from knowledge spill-overs: markets do not provide sufficient incentives for private investment in research because of the non-appropriable, public-good, intangible character of knowledge and its risky nature. New knowledge arising from R&D is non-rivalrous and only partially non-excludable: others may learn and use the knowledge, without necessarily paying for it. It is these spillovers that lead to social rates of return above private rates of return, and private investment levels below socially-desired levels. Divergence between social and private rates of return provides a reason for government intervention to increase private R&D investment to the higher socially-optimal level. It justifies in particular support for private R&D projects where the divergence between social and private returns is high. In an intangible economy that relies heavily on R&D investments by firms, governments therefore face difficult trade-offs. Industrial policy should encourage firms to invest in R&D by guaranteeing that they can enjoy the returns on their investments (for example through very strong intellectual property rights (IPR) systems), but the state should also encourage knowledge spillovers so firms can build on each other's innovations (which would weaken the case for strong IPR systems). A way to reconcile both objectives is for governments to engage in R&D themselves (for example, by funding universities). Another way to do so, as suggested by Haskel and Westlake (2018), is to develop IPR systems that are very clear and enforced, but not overly protective. In addition, public research is needed to meet specific public interest needs, providing common public goods which the market would not supply on its own, including defence, public health and a clean environment.

The coordination failure argument for industrial policy is based on the idea that many projects require simultaneous investment in different parts of the value chain. If different agents (eg downstream and upstream firms) make these investments, each individual investment might not be optimal for the overall value chain. This happens particularly for complex, early-stage projects with large externalities and significant information asymmetries. A critical question over the coordination failure argument for industrial policy is whether the government is able to solve this problem better than the market. Vertical integration or long-term contracts between intermediate and final-goods producers can help resolve coordination problems, although there are clearly limits to the extent to which firms can adjust to solve coordination problems, exemplified by the classic hold-up problem .

Perhaps the clearest case of market failure arises when information is lacking and/or different parties have different levels of access to it. Differences between investors and financiers in terms of access to information is a classic case that gives rise to capital market imperfections and impedes access to finance for lucrative investment projects. But parties in supply chains may also have different levels of access to information. Issues may also arise when there is incomplete information for everyone, such as for new projects in situations of high uncertainty. For new activities, entrepreneurs may simply not know what is profitable and what is not. In the presence of informational externalities, a free-rider problem arises between initial and subsequent investors. Early investors cannot recover their sunk costs when the outcome is unfavourable. But if it is unfavourable, this information on the profitability of the project spills over to others. If there is free entry *ex post*, no entrepreneur may be willing to make the initial investment and a socially beneficial market will not be established. Coordination problems are likely to further exacerbate the market-failure problem[5].

Industrial policy needs to address these market failures. In addition, industrial policy might help solve other contemporary economic issues associated with the growing intangible nature of economies, such as the increase in inequality, the productivity trap and secular stagnation (Haskel and Westlake, 2018). The growing importance of intangibles thus provides a new argument for industrial policy and increased state intervention.

---

5 This refers to a situation in which two parties may be able to work most efficiently by cooperating but refrain from doing so because each is concerned it might give the other party increased bargaining power and thus reduce its own profits.

4 New industrial policy

Critiques of the traditional, vertical-style industrial policies that prevailed during the 1960s and 1970s can be grouped into two larger clusters of arguments: on the capacity of bureaucrats and administrators to allocate public resources correctly to the market (by picking winners and subsidising them), and on the probability of rent seeking and 'capture'.

In terms of the first of these, the review of arguments for industrial policy in chapter 3 shows the enormous difficulties involved in implementing industrial policies. Policymakers would have to master an extraordinary range and depth of information and knowledge to implement policies successfully. Policymakers would have to be knowledgeable about firms and industries that generate knowledge spillovers, the relative amount of learning by individual firms from others and from their own experiences, the precise path of such learning over time and the magnitude of cost disadvantages at each stage in the learning process, and the extent to which early entrants generate benefits for future entrants. The breadth of knowledge and skills needed to implement an optimal policy would exceed that possessed by almost any institution, including the best consulting firms.

In addition, distortions could arise from lobbying efforts through which vested interests try to capture rents arising from public finances. Where accountability and transparency are lacking, pervasive lobbying efforts and corruption have resulted in inefficient and socially suboptimal allocation of rents. Altenburg *et al* (2015) give the examples of the German Renewable Energies Act[6] and of the EU emissions trading system[7] in this regard.

If the role of industrial policy is the creation of 'artificial' rents, the risks of capture, corruption and distortion are extremely tangible. This is a well-known issue, especially for countries with low institutional quality. Chang (2019) noted that the risk of political capture can also be the indirect product of different lobbying efforts, which can hinder the implementation of industrial policies. He cited the cases of Brazil, South Africa and other developing countries, where competing interests and lobbying groups (for example, the financial lobby pitted against the manufacturing lobby) have contributed to premature deindustrialisation. Because of greater pressure from the financial lobby, high interest rates in countries such as Brazil and South Africa undermined the competitiveness of the manufacturing sector. High (real) interest rates discourage investment in general, but impacts

6 The Renewable Energies Act established the principle of providing feed-in tariffs (over a 20-year period) for renewable sources of electricity generation (see the case study in section 6). The costs originating from guaranteed prices above market rates are translated into an electricity price surcharge borne by all electricity consumers, domestic and commercial. The result is thus a deliberate policy-induced rise in electricity costs. However, the law also foresees exemptions for particular types of companies. This is exactly where political capture kicks in. Such exemptions were initially confined to high energy-intensity manufacturers (electricity cost of at least 14 percent of production value) that were subject to international competition, such as steel and chemical companies. However, exemptions have proliferated and cover a broad range of diverse industries not foreseen under the provisions of the law. As a result, the sum total of exemptions grew from 7 percent of Germany's electricity consumption in 2004, to 20 percent in 2014. Initially well-defined and justified exemptions thus became the object of aggressive lobbying, leading to a level of political capture that erodes the credibility of the incentive. In late 2013, the European Commission opened an investigation into the compatibility of the exemptions with EU state aid rules, and the German government reformed the eligibility rules.

7 The emissions trading system has fallen prey to a mix of vested interests that advocate the free allocation of permits ('grandfathering'), exemptions and loopholes, and the excessive issuance of permits, resulting in windfall profits for polluting industries.

are particularly negative for investment in the manufacturing sector, where the requirement for borrowing is greater because of higher capital needs than in other sectors. These negative impacts of high interest rates on the manufacturing sector have clearly unfolded in Brazil and South Africa in the last two decades, with real interest rates frequently around 10-12 percent. As a consequence, few firms are able to borrow to invest (Andreoni and Chang, 2020).

Rent-seeking is likely to become increasingly challenging as firms rely more on intangible assets. Defending the ownership of, and appropriating the value from, intangible assets is much more complex than for tangible assets. Copyrights and patents are, in general, more subject to challenge than the ownership of, for instance, a production plant. All this may encourage firms to spend money on lobbying to protect their claims on intangible assets. Furthermore, the gains from such lobbying are typically greater for larger, incumbent firms because of the scalability of intangible assets. The resulting captured regulations may then discourage smaller firms from investing in intangible assets in the first place.

Even if optimal first-best policies were not possible because of the information and capture constraint, policy could still be efficient and effective. The effectiveness of industrial policy ultimately has to be evaluated on the basis of its realised outcomes compared to no intervention. In terms of realised outcomes, the history of industrial policy in Europe provides many examples of failures, such as the loss to the United States of the race to develop computers in 1960s and 1970s (when France implemented the *Plan Calcul*[8]), the loss to Japan of the

8   The *Plan Calcul* was a 1960s programme to promote a national or European computer industry, in response to concerns about French dependence on the US computer industry. Under it, an agency, a manufacturing company and a research institute were created, but it did not succeed in developing a French computer industry, and as of 1971, US firm IBM had a more than 50 percent market share in almost every European country. Under President Giscard d'Estaing, the *Plan Calcul* was progressively dismissed between 1975 and 1978, and ultimately deemed a failure.

race to develop semiconductors in the 1980s and 1990s, and the failure of Concorde, the British-French project to develop the first supersonic passenger aircraft[9]. Various failed programmes built the case for a laissez-faire approach to industrial policy. At a more systematic level, larger-scale evaluation studies most often have looked at the impact of trade protection, R&D subsidies and tax credits, and general subsidies. Also in these studies one can find cases – such as subsidies for specific industries or public procurement programmes – which have distorted the market, resulted in the picking of the wrong firms and have burdened the taxpayer with disappointing returns[10]. The big problem with evaluation studies is to identify the causal impact of industrial policy on outcomes, as proper counterfactuals to compare with are often lacking, and one has to take into account that policy interventions are not random but are implemented for a reason. More recent studies try to deal better with causal identification show that industrial policy can be effective in stimulating activities, but much depends, unsurprisingly, on the policies used and the institutional context.

Lacking robust evidence in support of industrial policy, and fully aware of the informational and rent-seeking issues that constrain the implementation of industrial policy, the literature has moved on with new insights to try to improve the design of industrial policy. A new wave of academic debate has arisen around new forms of industrial policy. This new industrial policy perspective, which started with the work of Rodrik (2014), is an attempt to move beyond the ideological division between state-driven intervention and purely market-based solutions. It argues for a smart combination of both. New industrial policy acknowledges both theoretical reasons for intervention, rooted

---

9   Concorde entered service in 1976 and operated for 27 years. During its development, the programme experienced huge overruns, delays and costs spikes. This impacted the commercial viability of the initiative, which was ultimately terminated in 2003.

10 For a review, see Noland & Pack (2003); Dechezleprêtre *et al* (2020), Rodrik (2004), Aiginger and Rodrik (2019); Aghion *et al* (2014).

in market failures, and the implementation difficulties (government failures). It addresses the information capacity of bureaucrats and political-capture arguments. What needs to be solved by industrial policy from this point of view (and what markets do when they function properly) is how to mobilise resources.

The new industrial policy perspective moves the debate away from the view of industrial policy as a set of tools to allocate resources, towards understanding it as a process. Rodrik (2014) argued for new industrial policy to be a *"process of institutionalised collaboration and dialogue rather than a top-down approach"* in which the government picks sectors or firms and transfers money to them. The private sector has to be one of the three fundamental stakeholders in this collaboration, in which the other two elements are the government and civil society.

Industrial policy should be designed in a way that makes it easier for the state to build policies based on the knowledge that resides in the private sector, while being legitimate from the point of view of civil society. The state's role should be to identify constraints and opportunities, in order to develop solutions that bring together private and public capacities and information, with aligned public and private motives, in a very pragmatic way. A modern framework should address the issues of rent-seeking and political capture, and all the inefficiencies and risks that lie at the intersection between the public and the private sectors, by effectively combining incentives and regulatory constraints, and building in accountability and transparency.

Rodrik (2014) posits three pillars for this theoretical framework: i) embeddedness; ii) discipline; iii) accountability[11].

The concept of embeddedness (or embedded autonomy) dates back to the work of Evans (1995). It starts from the notion that different stakeholders have specific characteristics, and that governments

---

11 This framework is also used in Altenburg and Rodrik (2017); Ambroziak (2017); Altenburg *et al* (2017); Andreoni and Chang (2019); Fernández-Arias *et al* (2020).

do not know in advance where market failures will occur. Therefore, government agencies have to be embedded with the private sector and have access to their information in order to leverage it to design policies. Embeddedness thus requires a high degree of collaboration between the public and private sectors, which would work closely to discover solutions. The design of public-private partnerships can take different forms. Deliberation councils, investment advisory councils, round tables, public-private venture funds and development banks are all examples through which governments can implement the embeddedness principle.

In the Rodrik interpretation, new industrial policies by definition assume that trust and competences can be developed over time. Embeddedness relies on a continuous, fair and open dialogue between the different stakeholders, something that could be defined as policy-learning. But while embedded, government agencies should not be 'in bed' with the private sector. The implementation of embeddedness must take into account informational asymmetries between different partners and how asymmetries change over time.

To avoid the risk of moving too slow or staying inactive in the face of the high uncertainties and high risks of failure, experimentation is crucial. Policies designed as learning experiments can help to reduce risks, provided that they are closely monitored and adjusted when new information arises. Monitoring will be required to deal with failures and mistakes. The instruments and tools used by industrial policy might initially not be the correct ones or might not work as planned. Testing and learning can offset these problems if built into the design of the policy. Governments should not start with the presumption that solutions are known, and industrial policy built on experimentation would ensure that the focus is no longer on 'picking winners', but much more on 'letting losers go' (Hallegatte *et al*, 2013). Openness to failure should be a characteristic of the design of industrial policy, which should incorporate uncertainty in its process. As Rodrik (2014) put it, *"failure is part and parcel of a successful industrial policy effort"*. A new industrial policy approach would therefore be a portfolio approach, with some initiatives within the initial portfolio failing along the way. A portfolio with no failures entails no risks.

While embeddedness and collaboration could represent a way to solve the information problem, they clearly entail the risk of capture and of provision of distorted information. To deal with the political-capture risk, industrial policy should include monitoring and transparency mechanisms, as well as mechanisms to align private and public incentives. To activate private agents and prevent 'cheating', proper incentives and accountability need to be in place.

Transparency on incentives and accountability mechanisms should be facilitated by roadmaps and clear government communication (Kemp and Never, 2017). A process of open policy dialogue should ensure a high degree of accountability. Accountability will be critical to the success or failure of industrial policy exercises.

Civil society will play an important role in new industrial policy (Bowles and Carlin, 2020). In the bottom-up policymaking which the embedded model involves, civil society including NGOs, trade unions, activist groups and citizen lobbying initiatives, must be as engaged as much as the private and public sectors in policy design.

The emphasis, within this new framework, on pragmatism, collaboration, embeddedness and accountability are inspired by experiences in Asia. Altenburg *et al* (2015) cited the examples of the industrial transformations in some Asian countries between the 1970s and the 1990s, highlighting a number of successful features in private-public alliances: the meritocracy of bureaucracies, the organisational capacity of the private sector, upward accountability of policymakers, competitive pressure, monitoring of sectoral performance, consumer protection and press freedom. Pragmatism overruled an ideological discussion in Singapore, when policymakers embraced very effectively and decisively plans for a free-trade economy, although 90 percent of the land in Singapore is state-owned (Chang, 2019). Japan and Korea are other examples of good incentive systems for all participants (companies, policymakers, administrators). Embedded autonomy worked well in safeguarding processes against lobbying. The success of those programmes relied on clear systems of incentives, in which performance indicators were clearly stated, as well as transparency requirements and serious evaluations conducted ex post for the firms targeted by the industrial policy programmes.

Competition as a feature for taming the government failure risk is reminiscent of Aghion *et al* (2011), who recommended competition and state-aid policy to foster the level-playing field within sectors. Any intervention should target those sectors with the greatest degree of within-sector competitiveness. A focus on competitiveness should be engrained in the public-private partnership mechanisms. Aghion *et al* (2015) found empirical evidence, for China, that industrial policy that subsidises firms can enhance productivity growth if the targeted firms within sectors are sufficiently competitive and innovative. The conclusions of Aghion *et al* (2011) were broadly endorsed by Altomonte and Veugelers (2019), who recommended a combination of horizontal measures ensuring competition and an innovation-friendly environment, with vertical measures that are careful about the choice of targeted firms and sectors, representing a portfolio approach to industrial policy, which should be coupled with competition-enhancing policies.

The discussions on principles for industrial policy design mostly focus on how to improve activities that already exist. Designing industrial policy for activities that do not yet exist is a very different challenge. Mazzucato (2011) made this point most vividly in what she defined as the 'entrepreneurial state'. The notion of the entrepreneurial state implies that not only should the state step into the economy, promote existing industries and solve their market failures, but also that government agencies should act as market creators. She furthermore proposed a broader *"mission-oriented"* approach to industrial policy (Mazzucato, 2018). The missions should be goals on which society agrees, taking into account its diverse range of stakeholders. The policies that direct economic and technical change should do so with the objective of reaching the goals. Broad acceptance of the missions would be rooted in citizen engagement, via multi-stakeholder consultations.

This system also implies setting concrete but ambitious milestones during the process. The United Nations' Sustainable Development Goals would be examples of missions, according to Mazzucato (2018). Meeting them requires a new toolkit that goes beyond fixing failures in existing markets. Strategic public investment in many different sectors should open up new industrial opportunities, to be developed further by the private sector. Mazzucato and Penna (2016) proposed a revived role for development banks as channels for entrepreneurial states. The public sector should help shape the industry by providing basic research innovations as bases for follow-up private investments. Examples are transistors and the internet. Gruber (2017) gave as an example IMEC (Interuniversity Microelectronics Centre), set up in Leuven, Belgium in 1982 by the Flemish government working with Flemish universities to strengthen the microelectronics industry in Flanders. IMEC is currently one of the most advanced research centres for nano-electronics, working in areas including sustainable energy.

Fernandez-Arias et al (2020) studied smart development banks[12] in more detail as facilitators of new activities within a new industrial policy perspective. Well-designed development banks can help governments discover where problems and failures lie. They should engage in the search for nascent economic activities that face obstacles from market or government failures. This requires intelligence gathering and dissemination of lessons learned rather than simply providing

---

12 Development banks are 'smart' when they *"identify market failures through their loan-screening and lending activities to guide their operations and provide critical inputs for the design of productive development policies. This intelligence role of development banks is similar to the role that modern theories of financial intermediation assign to banks as institutions with a comparative advantage in producing and processing information. However, while private banks focus on information on private returns, development banks would potentially produce and organise information about social returns"* (Fernandez-Arias et al, 2020).

credit. Development banks should transmit information on market and government failures to the relevant agencies. Fernandez-Arias *et al* (2020), in a survey of development banks, concluded that current practice is very far from what they propose. Nevertheless, they believe that development banks can be reoriented to exploit the complementarities between their lending and intelligence gathering.

5 A new green industrial policy

The new perspective on industrial policy elevates the industrial policy discussion out of the realm of strict economic goals such as competitiveness, productivity and GDP growth, to include broader societal goals. Societal goals involve climate stability, health, poverty prevention, the creation of quality jobs and reduced inequality. With climate as a societal goal to be included explicitly in the objectives of industrial policy, an industrial policy that is green follows naturally. How can policymakers design green industrial policies? What makes green industrial policy different from industrial policy and from climate policy? Here, we delve further into how the principles of industrial policy, and particularly of the new industrial policy perspective, can be applied in the design of green industrial policy.

5.1 A bold green industrial policy: urgency, risk-taking, experimentation

Dealing with climate crisis means tough targets. The decarbonisation challenge is both broad (it will have to be all-encompassing across the economy – this is where it differs from climate policy) and deep (it must achieve real carbon abatement, which is where it is different from industrial policy).

A feature of the climate crisis that is obvious but worth remarking is the absolute need for an urgent effort to mitigate it. The consequences in case of non-action would be devastating. As the Stern Review (2006) stated, *"The costs of stabilising the climate are significant but manageable; delay would be dangerous and much more costly"*. Fostering the greening of the economy is not only a strategic industrial move to achieve competitiveness, but a necessity to guarantee the continuation of society. For green industrial policy, more than for other areas of industrial policy, the lack of action and risk-taking can be particularly problematic in the long run, as scenarios of doing too little too late are extremely concerning. A green industrial policy portfolio with risks entails accepting failures. This puts the experimentation principle at the core of green industrial policy, going beyond the principle of only intervening if there is a clear case for intervention.

5.1.1 Public-private partnerships and civil society involvement

The huge transformative change of decarbonisation will require the involvement of the private sector and civil society more than in other areas of industrial policy. It will also require private-sector involvement. Public-private partnerships will be central to green industrial policy, much more than for climate policy, and will cover more private-sector activities than industrial policy.

5.1.2 Addressing green market failures: environmental externalities

The theoretical case for intervention is even more robust in the context of green industrial policies. In addition to classical market failures, environmental externalities must be dealt with because a clean environment represents a public good. Being characterised by broader market failures, green markets require more targeted support than non-green markets.

5.1.3 Green technology externalities

While the previously highlighted market failures argument applies to general industrial policies, some market failures are particularly relevant for green industries. Markets tend to underinvest in research and innovation, not only because of an aversion to risk and uncertainty, but also because of the spillover effects. Green technologies are often still early stage or emerging, with higher levels of risk and uncertainty. In addition, green technologies seem to be more complex than non-green technologies. Green technologies are a combination of a larger and more diverse set of technologies, compared to non-green technologies. Studies based on firm-level data (Ghisetti et al, 2015) and patent data (Barbieri et al, 2020) have found that green technologies are more complex than non-green technologies. In addition, Barbieri et al (2020) found that these technologies tend to have greater spillovers and cause effects in a wider variety of other domains. The greater risks and uncertainty, and the greater externalities from clean technologies, make the case for green industrial policy, calling for an approach that is more directed at supporting investment in clean technologies. The selection of tools and projects for green industrial policy should also be directed to those areas with the greatest clean market failures, where private and public returns diverge most.

5.1.4 Avoiding lock-ins and path dependencies
Beyond the spillover arguments, a push to invest in clean technologies is necessary to counter the locking-in of fossil fuel-based technologies and their path dependence (meaning the tendency for decisions to be made in the context of previous decisions, therefore perpetuating existing approaches). The difficulty in profiting from green technologies and in developing new low-carbon technologies is related to support for fossil fuel products given in different forms, from the absence of a sufficient carbon price to explicit fossil-fuel subsidies. This makes the private returns from non-green capital much higher than the returns it generates in terms of aggregate social welfare. As an indication of the magnitude of this issue, Coady et al (2019) estimated Europe's post-tax fossil-fuel subsidies at $261 billion in 2015. This happens because environmental externalities are not incorporated into the price of fossil fuels. In turn, lower-than-optimal fossil fuel prices make investment in green products relatively less profitable, reducing private incentives to invest green. These mechanisms can skew the market, not only in terms of production and technology adoption, but also in terms of innovation. Given the path-dependent nature of

innovation and its increased complexity and uncertainty in the green context, this market failure is particularly concerning, given the danger of locking-in industries or countries to unsustainable development paths based on 'dirty' technologies (Aghion *et al*, 2011, 2016). The case for subsidising green technologies, in this sense, is broader and stronger than the general case for alleviating R&D-related market failures. This is particularly relevant when considering that the cost of combating the climate crisis will increase substantially the more action is delayed. Locking-in unsustainable pathways will increase the cost of mitigating the climate crisis.

5.2 A balanced mix of green industrial policy instruments

Environment-directed industrial policy technology (innovation) cannot be neutral. It needs to make an *ex-ante* distinction between 'clean' and 'dirty' technologies and to choose 'clean' in order to address the greater knowledge externalities and lock-in risks. This still leaves the issue of how to choose between clean technologies. Even within green industrial policy, decisions must still be taken both vertically (eg choosing to focus on certain clean technologies, such as batteries or hydrogen) and horizontally (eg choosing which instruments to use, such as carbon prices, regulations, research subsidies, etc). Choices of clean technologies should be guided by the principle of divergence between expected social and private returns and the greatest scope for reducing clean market failures, while addressing sufficiently the governance failure challenges and avoiding risk-aversion. Choosing clean technologies should also take into account the spillovers of any choice for other non-selected clean technologies. This implies a good mix between vertical and horizontal instruments, support that is limited in time and the importance of ensuring fair competition (Aghion *et al*, 2011).

Kemp and Never (2017), on the basis of an examination of several green industrial policies in Europe, called for a mix of various policy instruments, with a balance (in timing and strength) of demand-pull instruments (such as public procurement) and technology-push instruments (such as tariffs or subsidies), to make policy as effective as possible. This points to a role for policy coordination and coherence in the green industrial policy mix.

5.3 A global green industrial policy: avoiding the tragedy of the commons

Climate change is a global commons problem. As stated by Edenhofer et al (2013), *"the atmosphere is a global common-pool resource in its function as a sink for greenhouse gases, and it is openly accessible and appropriated by everyone free of charge in most regions of the world".* The geographical origin of greenhouse gas emissions into the atmosphere has no effect on their impacts. Any jurisdiction taking action to limit emissions thus incurs the costs of its actions, while the benefits are distributed globally. Therefore, as noted by Aldy and Stavins (2011), *"for virtually any jurisdiction, the climate benefits it reaps from its actions will be less than the costs it incurs, despite the fact that the global benefits may be greater – possibly much greater – than the global costs."*

In economic theory terms, this problem is framed in terms of the famous tragedy of the commons (Hardin, 1968). The consequences of the tragedy of the commons are that all economic agents have an incentive to exploit a common good beyond the socially-optimal level, and they end up overexploiting it. There is also a free-riding issue that leads to underinvestment in solutions to this problem. Rodrik (2014) discussed the political economy and governance challenges emerging from this. He pointed out that, whereas environmental externalities on a micro-scale call for market correction, the bigger picture at the aggregate level can be understood in terms of coordination issues. Containing the global temperatures increase and reducing carbon emissions are, *per se*, global commons from which all countries can benefit. If this is not done, all countries can suffer the negative impact. In this sense, green industrial policy, like climate change policy, will have to be much more multilateral than traditional industrial policy.

Lütkenhorst *et al* (2014) pointed out the necessity, in this sense, of joint initiatives such as the Intergovernmental Panel on Climate Change (IPCC). Rodrik (2014) pointed out another political economy aspect of green industrial policy: the competitive motives of nation states. He argued that this can have both a positive and negative impact. It can be a zero-sum game, in which every resource invested to achieve a domestic advantage is at global cost, but these competitive motives can also spark a race for innovation that solves the market failures linked to price distortion (by lowering prices) and underinvestment in R&D. Global cooperation in R&D, particularly during pre-commercial phases, can bring about cost advantages, risk sharing and greater efficiencies from combining complementary knowledge and exploiting synergies. All this implies that multilateral coordination on green industrial policy should seek to achieve a good balance between cooperation and competition to reach global targets.

5.4 Addressing green industrial policy government failures

Most of the arguments against industrial policy deal with the practical implementation of industrial policy rather than its theoretical justifications. Criticisms about effective implementation remain valid for green industrial policy. How can green industrial policy avoid government failures while directing structural change in order to meet its goals?

The information problem is the first challenge. As a green industrial policy requires a more directed approach to clean technologies, it relies on the government having the information capacity to correctly allocate resources to the best sectors and players. The case of Solyndra, a US solar panel producer, illustrates well the extent of the information-capacity challenge faced by green industrial policy. Solyndra received production subsidies via US industrial policy programmes. While most of the solar-panel market was silicon-based, Solyndra relied on a different type of solar-panel material. Its competitive advantage was mostly due to the high price of silicon. The Barack Obama Administration pushed Solyndra as its green industrial policy champion. But when the price of silicon unexpectedly fell, and Solyndra could no longer compete with Chinese firms (it went bankrupt in 2011), the Obama Administration's intervention was criticised.

Another governance challenge is high uncertainty and the need for a long time horizon for green policymaking, conflicting with politicians' needs to find short-term successes. The difference in time horizons between policy planning and political cycles makes achieving coherent and sustained green industrial policy efforts extremely challenging. Green industrial policies thus need to be protected as much as possible from this problem of uncertainty and time inconsistency. A long-term vision of paths and objectives combined with milestones is important. Lütkenhorst *et al* (2014) highlighted the need for a social agreement on long-term roadmaps in order to prevent policies from becoming subject to political capture and the economy from being locked-in to unsustainable pathways. Measures could include investment guarantees and provision of long-term capital loans. Lütkenhorst *et al* (2014) also underlined the need to ensure flexibility under these different forward-looking settings. One example is feed-in tariffs that are guaranteed for 15 to 20 years: long-term prices are guaranteed, but the auctioning mechanism works in batches, in order to adapt to technology cost changes.

Viewing the climate change challenge as a societal transition to a new sustainable growth path, further increases the need for the broad involvement of stakeholders, including citizens. A broader set of stakeholders may exacerbate the rent-seeking challenge, but will also offset one another's rent-seeking incentives. To get citizens on board, Kemp and Never (2017) stressed the importance of communicating well the policies and their design. Altenburg *et al* (2017) quoted different examples of energy policy reforms undermined by a combination of *"strong opposition from interest groups"* and lack of broad societal consensus, especially in cases of strongly disruptive energy policies, such as the scrapping of fossil-fuel subsidies.

Kemp and Never (2017) also underlined the concept of *"embedded autonomy"* from the new industrial policy literature. When looking at Germany's national platform for electric mobility, for instance, they found the continuous involvement of different stakeholders (automobile producers, city planners, technology companies and environmental groups) was a key success factor. This transition also had a broad political support: it was backed by the Chancellor, and co-led by ministries. Kemp and Never (2017) concluded that broad political backing and the taking of responsibility gave more stability to the industrial policy programme. *"Embedded autonomy"* should also be associated with transparency, accountability and independence, in order to avoid political capture.

5.5 Summary: lessons for green industrial policy

Green industrial policy should have much bigger and broader objectives than typical industrial policy. Green industrial policy should address the meta-problems associated with the transformative change climate change brings, rather than seeking to boost the competitiveness of targeted sectors and firms. Its broadness is also different from climate change policy, which is more narrowly defined in terms of climate change targets. Longer-term broad objectives involving the whole of society should focus on building win-win coalitions, compared to the short-term competitiveness objectives of selected sectors and firms. This broader public interest is the foundation for the legitimacy of the policy. Objectives should be clearly identified and transparently, broadly and repeatedly communicated. Goals should be translated into clear, measurable targets and milestones, which are the basis of monitoring and evaluation.

Green industrial policy should activate and coordinate a broad set of stakeholders. From the private sector, various sectors and technologies and different parts of the value chain should be engaged in public-private partnerships. Future uncertainty about climate and technological scenarios underlines the importance of self-discovery on the market and industry-research-policy collaboration via forums, public-private partnerships or other means. However, this mechanism will have to be designed robustly to resist lobbying efforts and attempts at political capture.

A balanced set of incentives and constraints will be needed to promote sharing risks, information and resources (blended finance), while weeding out rent-seeking. Green industrial policy also requires citizen support and involvement.

The implementation of green industrial policy should be seen as a continuous learning process to deal with information problems and high uncertainties and risks. At the same time, the sense of urgency justifies policy action despite the high risks. In particular, green industrial policy should help to shape the landscape for new industrial eco-systems and markets, in which stakeholders still need to be connected for the first time. Intermediate instruments, such as smart development banks, and milestones may allow the risks of new, risky projects to be minimised. Green industrial policy should be open to policy experimentation. Experiments should have clear monitoring and evaluation plans, so that unsuccessful experiments are stopped or restructured in time.

It is clear that green industrial policy should deploy a broad mix of policy instruments, balancing horizontal and vertical policy instruments. Green industrial policy should set a clear direction towards 'clean' and away from 'dirty'. Selection within clean technologies should be based on proposed solutions for meeting the set targets. Bottom-up proposals should be chosen through competition. Co-financing should cover a balanced set of projects that accelerate and consolidate existing scientific and industrial capacities. Instruments should cover the whole value chain from research, development and diffusion, to manufacturing, distribution and sales (technology push, market pull).

These lessons make clear how critical the governance challenge will be for successful implementation of green industrial policy. Strong operational governance is needed to address coordination between the many different types of stakeholders, policy governance areas, instruments and projects, and to coordinate across different geographical layers. This requires competent, empowered governance bodies, which should be sufficiently politically independent or detached from political pressures, yet accountable for their achievements, with a set of clear, realistic milestones.

Both the market and the state are limited in what they can deliver. Successful green industrial policy will rest on mechanisms that make them work together efficiently. The design of public-private partnerships and strong policy governance are the basic foundations.

These lessons make it clear how critical the governance challenge will be for successful implementation of green industrial policy. Strong operational governance is needed to coordinate between the many different types of stakeholders, policy governance areas, instruments and projects, and to coordinate different geographical layers. This requires competent, empowered governance bodies, which should be politically independent or detached from political pressures, yet accountable for their achievements, with a set of clear, realistic milestones.

6 Green industrial policy in practice

We examine and assess the strengths and weaknesses of green industrial policy implemented in Germany, the Netherlands, Denmark and the United States.

6.1 Germany

Germany is often considered the textbook example of green industrial policymaking, because of its energy transition programme, *Energiewende*, which started in 2010 and is ongoing. A central part of this has been the introduction of a system of feed-in tariffs (FIT) to promote renewable energy.

Feed-in tariffs are one of the most common instruments of climate change policy. They guarantee to renewable electricity producers a fixed price above the market price. Typically, they are used to foster the deployment of solar and wind generation, and they involve long-term price fixing. This long-term price fixing reduces commercial uncertainty, increasing the incentives for deployment of renewables. However, successful deployment of these technologies does not necessarily imply success in their manufacturing, which might face technological risks and uncertainties.

There is clear evidence on the fact that during its initial phase (2010-2014), the outcome of the *Energiewende* policy programme was very different for the domestic solar panel manufacturing industry compared to the wind turbine industry. Lütkenhorst *et al* (2014) compared four different indicators of the impact: competitiveness, innovation, job creation and climate-change mitigation. On competitiveness, Germany's strong position in wind turbine manufacturing rather than solar panel manufacturing clearly shows up in export data (Figure 3). In terms of innovation, Germany ranked third in terms of the absolute number of green patents from 1990 to 2010, behind the United States and Japan. Figure 3 shows that there was little difference in the number of solar and wind patents and trends. Yet, between 1990 and 2010, Germany accounted for 21 percent of global wind technology patents, while for solar photovoltaic technology it only represented 12 percent. In terms of jobs, in 2012, solar and wind energy created 54 percent and 23 percent respectively of a total of 380,000 jobs attributed to renewable energies.

Figure 3: German net exports (€ millions) and numbers of wind/solar patents

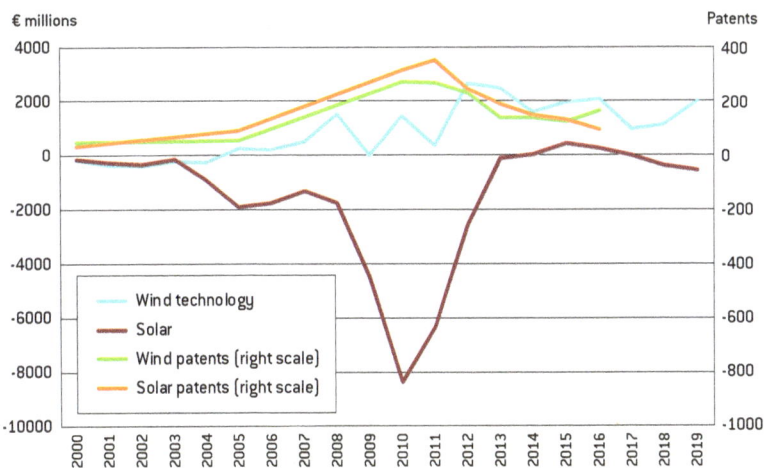

Source: Bruegel based on Patstat and Comtrade databases.

The solar panel industry's weaker overall performance is mainly due to strong Chinese competition and the lack of an accommodating industrial policy. Feed-in tariffs provided an important boost in demand for solar panels in Germany. The government guaranteed these tariffs for 20 years, so risk and uncertainty were considerably reduced, creating a stable investment environment and readiness on the part of capital markets to finance renewable energy projects at relatively low interest rates. But no direct support was given to the panel manufacturing industry. Insufficient attention was therefore paid to making the industry innovative, developing the latest cost-efficient technologies and competing at the technological frontier with Chinese manufacturers. Chinese manufacturers, who enjoyed a general manufacturing cost advantage compared to Germany, and could access huge credit lines with very low interest rates, were the major beneficiaries from the market that the German feed-in tariffs created. The *Paris Tech Review* (2012) noted *"expansion was put above upgrading"*. The *Paris Tech Review* editors argued that if creating a national competitive industry is the objective, it is vital to also support R&D in the local manufacturing sector.

Wind turbines are different. The wind turbine industry is more established industry than solar panels in Germany, which (like other European countries) has managed to develop a solid wind sector, in particular because of German technological know-how in the field of mechanical engineering, and because of weaker competition from Chinese and other international players. Moreover, Germany's turbine manufacturers, specialised component suppliers, wind park operators and research institutions (more than 300 partners in total) are clustered in the same region, supported by local governments. This has facilitated the knowledge spillovers and coordination mechanisms required for highly knowledge intensive industries.

The German solar energy case makes it clear that the deployment of climate change policy instruments (in this case feed in tariffs) is not necessarily sufficient from a green industrial policy perspective. So, should solar energy be considered a green industrial policy failure in Germany? The policy implications are not so straightforward. Although Germany failed to create a competitive solar panel manufacturing industry, it should be considered where the real social value added lays in this industry. End users of solar panels benefitted from the feed-in tariffs, as did suppliers and workers, as the industry is characterised by a high density of installation and maintenance jobs. To the extent that FIT made this part of the solar panels value chain more attractive, an overall positive social welfare outcome was realised, even without explicit strong domestic solar panel manufacturers or support for explicit policy intervention in favour of manufacturing.

Surprisingly, the rapid deployment of renewables in Germany did not lead to lower total greenhouse gas emissions but rather to stagnation. Electricity prices fell considerably as a result of oversupply, resulting from unexpectedly high generation from renewable sources. Low input prices and the low carbon price in the EU emissions trading system exacerbated the situation. Therefore, at times, only the cheapest energy sources remained competitive: hard coal and, in particular, lignite in the case of Germany (Lütkenhorst *et al*, 2014).

The *buildings energy efficiency* part of Germany's energy transition programme, meanwhile, was based on three pillars: regulation, fiscal incentives and a high level of transparency to stakeholders and markets (Kemp and Never, 2017). The policy was gradually introduced by raising buildings energy efficiency standards, to overcome the various imperfections in the real estate and construction markets. Market failures included unequal access to information, split incentives between tenants and owners in terms of energy efficiency and mispricing of future energy costs at the time of construction (Kemp and Never, 2017). As we have discussed, these situations call for collaboration and policy learning, in which targets are progressively adapted. In terms of public-private partnerships, buildings energy-efficiency agencies were set-up in Germany to check and expand the policy framework and promote experimental measures. Agencies were also responsible for the evaluation and monitoring of ongoing programmes. Weiß *et al* (2014) performed an economic assessment, concluding that the policy managed to reduce buildings' energy consumption and also *"impacted the regional value chain by €14 billion and generated about 287,000 full time jobs"*. El-Shagi *et al* (2014) concluded that regulation had a strong indirect impact on innovation. Key success factors are identified in the process of continuous revision of regulation and incentives, in the combination of different types of measures, in the collaboration between different participants and in the promotion of complementary measures, such as the use of renewable energy in buildings.

The *Energiewende* case makes it clear that climate change policy instruments, such as feed-in tariffs, although important for supporting renewable energy, may not be sufficient from the perspective of green industrial policy, which requires more focus on innovation, job creation and competitiveness, particularly for infant renewable energy sectors. Looking at the broader picture of the energy system in Germany, Lütkenhorst *et al* (2014) made three recommendations. First, Germany has a fragmented multi-level institutional framework, that despite its reputation, needs to be pooled together politically to efficiently tackle the problem. Second, green policies must interact with other policies, including those at the European level, avoiding duplication, and working towards common goals, however politically difficult this may be. Third, it is necessary to be pragmatic in alliances for this transformation with very different stakeholders. Schwarz (2020) argued that, in the German context, citizen involvement should be taken into consideration and framed properly, given that citizens are often the unrecognised stakeholders during these policy processes. Civil society needs to be fully recognised as a stakeholder in green industrial policy and is neither less nor more important than the private and public sectors. Acceptance of industrial policy and transitions is a key element that in the future will likely interact with different macro-trends.

6.2 Netherlands

The Netherlands provides another interesting case study for Europe. Kemp (2010) labelled the spirit of the programmes that started in 2002, as a *"guided evolution"*, by means of experimentation and a portfolio approach, with an emphasis on knowledgeable players. Kemp and Never (2017) defined the Dutch approach as a systemic green industrial policy, building on the transition management literature. The Dutch approach in phasing-in green technologies considered the entire energy system. In order to achieve the goals, the economic affairs ministry and the environment ministry were brought closer together to jointly manage the framework programme. The framework involved the establishment of several different transition platforms, the drafting of action plans and different scenarios. As Kemp (2010) outlined, the process was designed so that *"individuals from the private and the public sector, academia, and civil society come together to develop a common ambition for particular areas, develop pathways, and identify useful transition experiments"*. These experiments involved R&D programmes for technology support and the creation of networks of expertise. Kemp and Never (2017) showed in practice an example of what Rodrik (2014) defined as self-discovery or embeddedness: the set-up, in 2004, of a *"front-runners desk"* designed to *"help innovative companies with problems encountered and to help policy to become more innovation friendly"*. Private-sector knowledge informed policy about problems such as credit constraints. It is interesting to note that in order to foster the energy transition in the country, the Dutch regulator also devised a 'regulatory sandbox'[13]. Aimed at promoting decentralised, sustainable electricity generation, this initiative allowed homeowners' associations and energy cooperatives to propose projects that were prohibited by current regulation. In particular, local experimenters could organise peer-to-peer supply and determine their own tariffs for energy transport in order to localise, democratise and decentralise energy provision.

Despite the good characteristics of the policy design, the evaluation of all these initiatives in terms of efficiency and effectiveness remains difficult. Kemp (2010) identified the electric mobility sector as

---

13 A framework set up by a regulator to allows start-ups and other innovators to conduct live experiments in a controlled environment under a regulator's supervision.

a success in terms of transition management, while the effects on the energy sector were less clear. Kemp and Never (2017) also pointed to policy inconsistency, as the energy market went through a programme of liberalisation. This lack of consistency in policy targets watered down the effectiveness of the transition management programmes.

6.3 Denmark

Denmark is interesting for its specific experience in the wind turbine industry. Denmark has been a pioneer in wind energy production at global level (Figure 4).

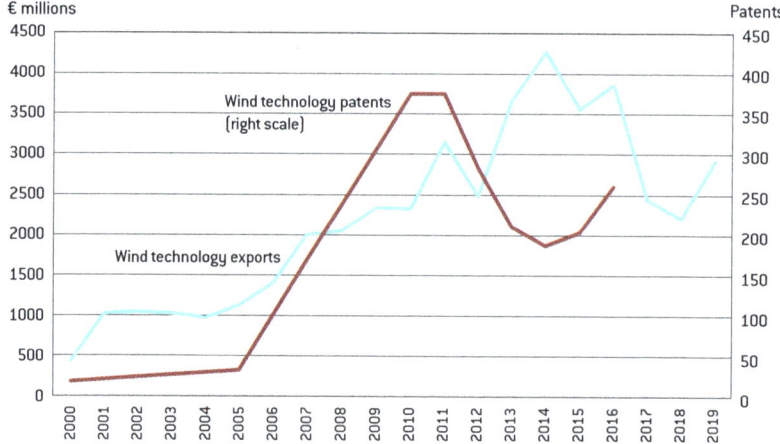

Figure 4: Danish net exports (€ millions) and patents, wind energy

Source: Bruegel based on Patstat and Comtrade databases.

The elements of Denmark's green industrial policies have to be understood in the context of specific ownership structures, based on cooperatives. Cooperatives became more and more important from the 1970s, as Danish wind companies moved from family-owned structures to a world-leading industry. This development *"was driven from the bottom-up, with enthusiasts influencing the political process in such a way that government got engaged in providing the enabling conditions to boost the development of the sector, through economic incentives and favourable ownership restrictions"* (Mendonça and Lacey, 2009).

Mendonça and Lacey (2009) linked this structure to the idea of *"innovative democracies"*, which is defined by Hvelplund (2005) as *"the active collaboration of a number of actors, including politicians, new small private firms, the energy companies and the grassroots energy movement"*. Clearly, this model presents some of the features of the theoretical framework for green industrial policy (section 5). This approach is characterised by a combined bottom-up and top-down approach that includes the private and public sectors, civil society, activists and NGOs. This spread of involved parties has helped counterbalance lobbying efforts by fossil-fuel companies.

Two sets of government policies further contributed to wind industry developments in Denmark. The Danish government implemented several programmes of feed-in tariffs, which stayed relatively stable from the 1980s to the beginning of the 2000s. In addition, R&D and investment subsidies had a positive impact on the production and deployment of wind turbines, as shown by Klaassen *et al* (2005). This highlights the importance of a balanced mix of policy instruments, particularly the interplay between demand-pull and technology-push green industrial policy tools. More recent work by Cook and Lin Lawell (2020) has confirmed empirically the success of feed-in tariff schemes, as well as another Danish government programme: the replacement certificate programme, which provided incentives for the replacement of old turbines.

In institutional and political economy terms, an important part of the success of the Danish model has been its persistency (Mendonça and Lacey, 2009). We can think of the Danish model as a clear way to address the market failures linked to uncertain time horizons. Continuous involvement of NGOs, academics and citizens in the policy process, in the innovative democracy model (as also referred to by Schwarz, 2020), ensures that the risk of doing too little is mitigated by the involvement of stakeholders who keep the pressure to act constant.

6.4 United States

Green industrial policy in the United States was strengthened after the 2008 economic crisis with the 2009 American Reinvestment and Recovery Act, and subsequently with the Climate Action Plan (2013) (Rodrik, 2014). The main instruments deployed were loan guarantees and tax incentives. Rodrik (2014) discussed the case study of solar-panel producer Solyndra (see section 5.8), as an illustration of failing industrial policy. Rodrik (2014) stressed that necessarily some of the companies targeted by industrial policy will fail along the way, while only a few will be hits – Tesla is one example. Rodrik (2014) proposed to look at industrial policy as a portfolio of investments. From an analysis of the US National Research Council (NRC) which evaluated, based on a portfolio approach, programmes carried out by the US Department of Energy (DOE) (including R&D projects), Rodrik (2014) concluded that at the portfolio level, the net benefits surpassed the net losses. He also stressed the need to understand and avoid political capture. The NRC highlighted how much of value added in industrial policy efforts came from relatively modest projects.

The DOE and the Advanced Research Projects Agency – Energy (ARPA-E) are the US public agencies most widely analysed in the framework of industrial policy studies. They are considered, together with the US Defense Advanced Research Projects Agency (DARPA), as good examples of state industrial policy efforts resulting in breakthrough scientific advancements (including microprocessors, space missions and the internet). But what characterises the approach of these agencies? Evaluations (which are empirically difficult) of these types of agencies and programmes show that their success has more to do with the design of the institution and policies, the quality of the people involved and operating market conditions, rather than their budgets.

Goldstein and Narayanamurti (2018) estimated the effectiveness of public funding of DOE and ARPA-E in stimulating the production of research and patents. While DOE categorises funding into basic or applied research, ARPA-E has a more flexible approach, which better fits energy research. In addition, ARPA-E seems to address purposefully uncertainty, as the selection of projects favourably takes into account their disruptive – and thus uncertain – nature (Rodrik and Sabel, 2019). ARPA-E has a form of governance that puts its own design under review, with gradual and incremental changes based on continuous monitoring. The evidence suggests that the impact of ARPA-E, in which science advancement, in parallel to technology advancement, is stimulated more, has been broader than the impact of the DOE in general. Goldstein and Narayanamurti (2018) concluded that *"in order for DOE to fulfil its energy mission, it must fund research in a way that allows science and technology to coexist with minimal friction between them"*. Rodrik (2019) added that the ARPA-E approach is successful in eliminating gaps in technical knowledge. These spaces are exactly the overlaps between science and technology discussed by Goldstein and Narayanamurti (2018).

6.5 Lessons learned

A first lesson from these four green industrial policy cases is the importance of effective collaboration between all parts of society. Two areas that stand out are citizens and private industry. Citizens ultimately must accept policies, while private industry contributes significant knowledge and expertise. Policy should be able to involve both industry and society as new industrial policy advocates. Best practices in this respect have been seen in both the Netherlands and Denmark. In the Netherlands, transition pathways have long been negotiated by all stakeholder groups, enabling constructive collaboration (this has been done with the 2019 Dutch National Climate Agreement of the Netherlands, the *Klimaatakkoord*). In Denmark, cooperative ownership structures and bottom-up political activism have been crucial to the successful wind industry. Public-private partnerships have enjoyed similar success in Germany.

Another lesson is the importance of policy stability, commitment and predictability over a longer term horizon. The development of the Danish wind industry was supported strongly by stable and sensible policies. Conversely, literature has noted that policy inconsistency in the Netherlands, arising from energy market liberalisation programmes, reduced the effectiveness of transition-management programmes. Yet, in view of high levels of uncertainty, long-term commitment needs to go hand in hand with flexibility. Though built on a stable platform, policies are gradually adapted and strengthened over time. Effective stakeholder engagement allows this to be done in an informed manner. The German experience of progressively adapted targets for energy efficiency in buildings is a good example.

Measures should mix demand-pull and technology-push, general, horizontal instruments, and specific, targeted instruments. On selecting targets, the US experience with Solyndra shows that public administrations should refrain from placing any one industry or organisation on a pedestal, and should instead reinforce the message that a successful industrial policy is characterised by risk taking involving winners but also losers. Political communication must reinforce this message.

A final observation from the German experience of feed-in-tariffs is the importance of clearly defining and understanding the relative importance of 'green' and 'industrial policy'. The German FIT arguably catalysed the global market for solar panel, yet German players have a relatively low share of the market. From a purely industrial policy perspective, the conclusion might be that this was a failure. But from a green perspective, the policy was successful. Even from an industrial policy perspective it was a success, at least when taking a broader view, including the benefits of value added and jobs created in the servicing of solar panels. The Danish wind deployment programme was successful from both the sectoral and broader perspectives.

7 Green industrial policy in the European Union

7.1 The status of green industrial policy in the EU

Table 1 on the next page provides an overview of the status of green industrial policy in Europe. It illustrates how Europe remains far from having a fully-fledged green industrial policy. Instead, there is a multitude of green industrial policy initiatives, covering various policy competences and different geographical layers (regional, national and EU). These initiatives are generally not coordinated, and may even conflict. This is a major issue, because significantly different green industrial policies in different countries fragment the EU single market and could undermine the level playing field. Strong EU action and coordination is justified.

Table 1: Europe's green industrial policy landscape

	Innovation and technology	Investments and deployment	Framework conditions
EU level	Framework programmes (Horizon Europe); European Innovation Council; Missions; EU Innovation Fund (section 7.3.4)	EU budget and Next Generation EU; European Investment Bank (section 7.3.5); Single market rules (eg green public procurement) (section 7.3.7)	Coordination of national green industrial policies (eg European Semester; RIS3; IPCEIs) (sections 7.3.1 and 7.3.3);Competition policy; Environmental standards; Climate policy (eg carbon price, renewable and energy efficiency targets, clean standards; section 7.3.6); Development policy (7.3.8); Monetary policy
National level	Public R&D spending; Intellectual property protection law (at EU level)	Government investment programmes, incentives, subsidies, public procurement, clean energy standards	Consistency of macroeconomic policies with industrial strategy; Climate targets; Environmental standards; Environmental taxation
Regional level	Implementation of public-private partnership in place-based setups (eg university-industry collaborations)	Smart specialisation strategies; Regional Investment budgets; Implementation of EU Cohesion policies	Regulations (such as buildings energy efficiency)

Source: Bruegel.

EU regions promote their own 'smart specialisation'[14] initiatives in order to exploit their existing competitive advantages or to establish a competitive advantage in certain green technology sectors (eg solar panels, batteries, wind turbines – or related components). The EU regional policy framework incentivises regions to design and implement research and innovation strategies for smart specialisation through the so-called RIS3 programme[15]. Bergamini and Zachmann (2020) showed that low-carbon products tend to be concentrated in certain European regions, such as Rhône-Alpes in France, Dresden and Stuttgart in Germany, and Lombardy in Italy. The question is whether an alignment of these regional policies with national and EU policy is possible, to exploit cross-regional synergies.

EU countries and regions often use different policy tools to push their green industrial policies, ranging from public funding to subsidies for the deployment of green technologies, from green public procurement to clean energy standards.

At EU level, there are also several policies that can be used for green industrial policy, including competition policy, climate policy, research and innovation policy, EU public investments, EU single market rules and development policy. The following sections review in more detail the EU's industrial policy approach and the main green industrial policy tools deployed at EU level.

14 'Smart specialisation' is an innovation policy concept that aims to boost regional innovation, contributing to growth and prosperity by helping and enabling regions to focus on their strengths. The concept is based on partnerships between businesses, public entities and knowledge institutions.

15 The RIS3 (Regional Integrated Smart Specialisation Strategies) programme is an EU Cohesion Policy tool that supports the creation of knowledge-based jobs and growth in leading research and innovation hubs, and in less-developed and rural regions.

7.2 The European Commission's 'New industrial strategy for Europe' and its green aspect

In February 2019, France and Germany sparked a lively debate by publishing 'A Franco-German manifesto for a European industrial policy fit for the 21st century' (BMWi, 2019). The manifesto was based on a simple idea: at a time of increasing global competition, Europe must pool its strengths to remain a global manufacturing and industrial power. To do so, the manifesto called for a new approach to EU industrial policy, notably based on a revision of EU competition rules (including a revision of merger guidelines and relaxation of state-aid rules), the implementation of protective measures to safeguard European technologies and companies, and funding for disruptive innovation.

In March 2020 – as COVID-19 started to bite in Europe – the European Commission then published a plan for a 'New industrial strategy for Europe' (European Commission, 2020a)[16], a strategy primarily aimed at *"managing the green and digital transitions and avoiding external dependencies in a new geopolitical context"*, to use the words of EU Internal Market Commissioner Thierry Breton. The main underpinnings of the strategy were: i) the need to face emerging global competitors and promote Europe's 'strategic autonomy'; ii) the need to cope with a period of global economic uncertainty; and iii) the need to face the twin ecological and digital transitions.

The strategy encompasses a number of areas, from intellectual property to public procurement, but focuses mainly on competition policy. In line with the Franco-German manifesto, the EU strategy calls for EU competition rules to be reviewed, including a revisiting of state-aid rules and a revision of EU instruments on foreign subsidies.

Being more general, the EU new industrial strategy is not a green industrial strategy, but it does contain an explicit green aspect. The

---

16 It should be noted that the European Commission publishes industrial policy strategies regularly. See European Commission (2010, 2012, 2014, 2017).

strategy actually never uses the expression 'green industrial policy' but a set of green goals is specified: i) securing the supply of clean energy and raw materials; ii) stepping up investment in green research, innovation, deployment and up-to-date infrastructure; and iii) creating lead markets in clean technologies through regulatory policies, public procurement and competition policy.

The strategy outlines a set of green policy action areas: i) support for zero-carbon steelmaking; ii) launch of a chemicals strategy for sustainability; iii) launch of an energy efficiency 'renovation wave'; iv) creation of an EU Just Transition Fund; v) launch of a clean hydrogen strategy; and vi) development of a carbon border adjustment mechanism.

The need for public-private partnerships and for coordination between EU countries and regions is also explicitly recognised: *"EU institutions, Member States, regions, industry and all other relevant players should work together to create lead markets in clean technologies and ensure our industry is a global frontrunner"*. The strategy also recognises the need for the EU to leverage the impact, size and integration of its single market.

All in all, the strategy appears more as a collection of more-or-less novel energy, climate, innovation and social policy initiatives, rather than as a truly coherent green industrial policy framework. On this basis, the measures outlined in the strategy seem unlikely to create the necessary framework to really turn the green transition into an industrial opportunity for Europe. Some general elements that reflect the 'new industrial policy' approach (such as the idea of pushing industrial ecosystems encompassing all players operating in a value chain; see the discussion of European Alliances in section 7.3.2) are in the direction of green industrial policy, but much stronger action is required to develop a workable, effective EU green industrial policy (chapter 8).

7.3 The EU's main green industrial policy tools

7.3.1 Coordination of national green industrial policies: the European Semester and smart specialisation programmes

There is a real need for better coordination of EU countries' respective national green industrial policies, in order to prevent distortions of the EU single market and to enable synergies and economies of scale. Strong EU coordination in the field is thus of paramount importance, particularly if Europe wants to establish itself at the frontier of green technology and green technology value added creation.

To coordinate the various green industrial policy initiatives underway at national and regional levels, the EU can leverage the national reform programmes developed within the European Semester and the regional RIS3 smart specialisation programme. In other words, the broad EU green industrial policy framework should become embedded in the member-state national reform programmes and regions' smart specialisation programmes. Regular evaluation of these programmes should be done by the Commission, with evaluation helping in the coordination of national industrial policy initiatives. This is even more important today, as the European Semester becomes more relevant than before given its central role in the governance of the EU post-COVID-19 recovery plan, Next Generation EU.

7.3.2 European Alliances

Another EU instrument for green industrial policy is European public-private partnerships or joint projects or alliances: European Alliances, as done for batteries in 2017 (Box 1) and for clean hydrogen in 2020 (Box 2).

Inspired by the Airbus consortium, these European Alliances are aimed at creating European integrated, cross-border value chains in technologies that are considered central for the future of the energy transition. The goal is twofold: to seize the job, growth and investment potential of new green technologies, and to prevent technological dependence on the EU's competitors.

In practice, these alliances are networks of the main industrial and innovation players (including SMEs), regional authorities, national authorities, the European Commission and the European Investment Bank. Importantly, projects developed in this context can receive state aid from EU countries (see section 7.3.3 on the Important Projects of Common European Interest) and are therefore channels through which the EU level can support national or regional green industrial policy.

Box 1: The European Battery Alliance

Launched in 2017, the European Battery Alliance supports the development of highly innovative and sustainable technologies for lithium-ion batteries with longer lifetimes and shorter charging times, and that are safer and more environmentally friendly than those currently available. The Alliance promotes research and development across the batteries value chain, from mining and processing of raw materials, production of advanced chemical materials, design of battery cells and modules and their integration into smart systems, and recycling and repurposing of used batteries (European Commission, 2020b). More specifically, the Alliance focuses on:

1. Securing access to raw materials for batteries from resource-rich countries outside the EU, facilitating access to European sources of raw materials, and improving access to secondary raw materials obtained through recycling;
2. Supporting scaled-up European battery cell manufacturing and a full competitive value chain in Europe. The Alliance brings key industry players and national authorities together and works in partnership with EU countries and the European Investment Bank to support large-scale, integrated (cross-border) manufacturing projects;
3. Strengthening industrial leadership through accelerated research and innovation support to advanced (eg lithium-ion) and frontier (eg solid state) technologies;

4. Developing and strengthening a highly skilled workforce along the whole value chain. This includes providing adequate training, re-skilling and upskilling, and making Europe attractive for world-class experts in the field;
5. Supporting the sustainability of EU battery cell manufacturing industry with the lowest environmental footprint possible. This entails setting requirements for safe and sustainable battery production in Europe;
6. Ensuring consistency with the broader EU regulatory and enabling framework (including the clean energy strategy and mobility packages, and trade policy).

In December 2019, the European Commission approved under EU state aid rules an Important Project of Common European Interest jointly notified by Belgium, Finland, France, Germany, Italy, Poland and Sweden that will support activities in the framework of the European Battery Alliance. This public funding support amounts to approximately €3.2 billion, which is expected to unlock an additional €5 billion in private investment. The completion of the projects supported by this public funding is planned for 2031 (European Commission, 2019a).

Box 2: The European Clean Hydrogen Alliance

Launched in 2020 as part of the 'New industrial strategy for Europe', the European Clean Hydrogen Alliance aims to support the deployment of hydrogen technologies by 2030, bringing together renewable and low-carbon hydrogen production, demand in industry, mobility and other sectors, and hydrogen transmission and distribution. With this initiative, the EU seeks to become a global leader in this nascent domain.

The Alliance aims to expand from 500 companies in 2020 to 1000 companies in 2024. Its main target is a level of 6 gigawatt (GW) of clean hydrogen by 2024, and then 40 GW (EU) and 40 GW (non-EU) clean hydrogen by 2030 (European Commission, 2020c). This process is ongoing, and relevant Important Project of Common European Interest have yet to be approved at time of writing.

7.3.3 Important Projects of Common European Interest

Competition policy possibly represents the most potent green industrial policy tool the EU has at its disposal, as it regulates interventions in the market by EU countries. Unsurprisingly, competition policy was at the centre of the pan-European discussions in 2019 around the need for a new green and digital industrial policy for Europe.

A revisiting of EU competition rules should indeed be an important part of developing an EU green industrial policy, as long as the application of competition rules is not just aimed at a 'negative coordination', in which all countries are permitted to intervene in the market as they prefer. Instead there should be a 'positive coordination', in which countries can jointly act in certain green technologies, internalising externalities and exploiting synergies.

An example of 'positive coordination' is the Important Projects of Common European Interest (IPCEI), a tool introduced in 2014 (European Commission, 2014) in the context of a wider modernisation of state-aid rules (European Commission, 2012). In essence, countries can provide state aid to particular projects (ICPEI) if they meet the following conditions: i) contribute to strategic EU objectives; ii) involve several EU countries; iii) involve private financing by the beneficiaries, iv) generate positive spillover effects across the EU; and v) are highly ambitious in terms of research and innovation. Both the European Batteries Alliance and the European Clean Hydrogen Alliance (Boxes 1 and 2) are IPCEI, but more are in the pipeline.

7.3.4 Innovation policy

In general terms, Europe's R&D spending in relation to GDP remains lower than that of other major economies. In 2017, Europe's private and public sectors combined spent 2.06 percent of GDP on R&D, compared to 2.07 percent in China, 2.8 percent in the US, 3.2 percent in Japan and 4.5 percent in South Korea (Eurostat, 2020). Europe will thus not meet the target it set itself in 2010 to spend 3 percent of GDP on R&D by 2020. The EU business enterprise sector in particular needs to invest more. Its share of total R&D expenditure is much lower in Europe (64 percent) than in the US (72 percent), or China, Japan and South Korea (almost 80 percent) (Eurostat, 2019).

Europe invests less in climate-related R&D than the United States and China (Figure 5). In particular, Europe is not well-positioned in the fast-growing technologies, ranging from electronics to digital sectors, which will increasingly underpin clean energy, clean mobility and smart buildings. To truly develop a green industrial policy, the EU must push the business enterprise sector to scale-up its R&D investment in these sectors.

Figure 5: Investment in climate-related R&D, 2011-2018 (€ billions)

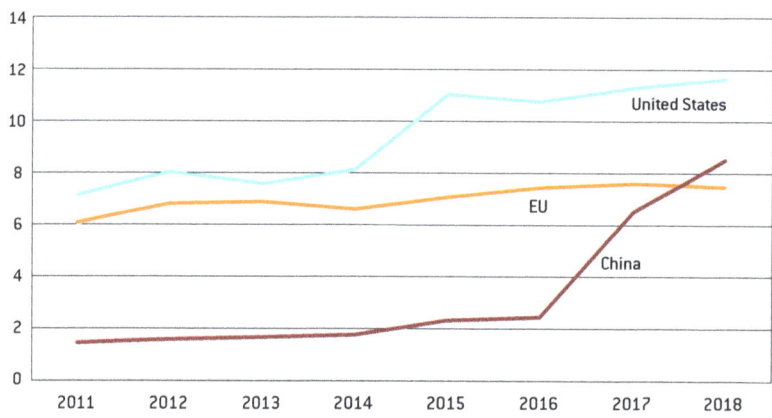

Source: Bruegel based on Bloomberg New Energy Finance.

Most of the public budget for clean technologies is at the level of member states and regions. Nevertheless, the EU level can complement and leverage national and regional public investments as well as private investments. The EU has at its disposal various tools to do so: i) its research and innovation framework, called Horizon Europe for the period 2021-2027, particularly with its Missions and the European Innovation Council components; ii) the EU Innovation Fund, developed in the framework of the EU emissions trading system (ETS); iii) the European Institute of Innovation and Technology.

Of Horizon Europe's budget of close to €100 billion, 35 percent has been allocated to actions aimed at tackling climate change. More generally there is a commitment to use the overall programme to help achieving the United Nations Sustainable Development Goals and to boost EU competitiveness and growth (European Commission, 2019b). Missions and the European Innovation Council are two novel elements in Horizon Europe.

Three out of the five Missions relate to climate change (Box 3 on the next page). These can be considered green industrial policy tools, while also responding to the need to create institutionalised processes of collaboration between institutions, civil society and the private sector.

The European Innovation Council (EIC) was created in 2017 as a pilot initiative within Horizon 2020 to fund the most talented radical innovators and help their companies scale up and expand beyond European borders. It was given a budget of around €3 billion for the period 2018-2020, and will be fully implemented from 2021 under Horizon Europe. The EIC could become an important green innovation tool, with a strong mandate in the areas of clean energy, clean mobility and smart buildings.

Box 3: Horizon Europe Missions

Inspired by the Apollo 11 mission to put a man on the moon, Horizon Europe Missions aim to tackle some of the greatest global challenges, within certain timeframes and budgets. The European Commission involves civil society in the design, monitoring and assessment of the Missions. Five expert boards were set up to define missions covering cancer, climate adaptation, healthy oceans and seas, climate-neutral cities and soil health (for further information, see https://ec.europa.eu/info/horizon-europe/missions-horizon-europe_en). In September 2020, the boards proposed the five more specifically-defined Missions:

1. Conquering Cancer: Mission Possible. Aimed at preventing more than 3 million premature deaths by 2030.
2. A Climate Resilient Europe. Aimed at preparing Europe for climate disruptions and accelerating the transformation to a climate resilient and just Europe by 2030.
3. Mission Starfish 2030: Restore our Ocean and Waters. Aimed at cleaning up marine and fresh waters, restoring degraded ecosystems and habitats and decarbonising the blue economy by 2030.
4. 100 Climate-Neutral Cities by 2030, by and for the citizens. Aimed at supporting, promoting and showcasing 100 European cities in their systemic transformations to climate neutrality by 2030, and turning these cities into innovation hubs.
5. Caring for Soil is Caring for Life. Aimed at promoting good practices to make at least 75 percent of all soils healthy for food, people, nature and climate by 2030.

Selected missions will start to be implemented in 2021 as part of Horizon Europe.

The EIC is split into two branches: the EIC Accelerator and the EIC Pathfinder. The Pathfinder supports breakthrough research projects with grants of up to €4 million. The Accelerator supports SMEs that have new ideas and the potential to scale up. This instrument has a fund of up to €15 million in grants and equity. The EIC Accelerator includes more than 5,500 firms[17]. Of these 922 (17 percent) are in energy and 424 in transportation (8 percent). In 2020, the first call for projects was opened by the Accelerator programme with a focus on green objectives. The European Commission has identified 38 projects

---

17 This portfolio includes projects that received funding previously under the EU's SME Instrument. Approximately 71 percent of projects in the portfolio received a €50,000 grant under the SME Instrument scheme.

through this call (European Commission, 2020d), which will receive both a grant and equity investment. The Pathfinder branch at time of writing covers 431 funded projects. Of these, 15 percent are in the areas of energy and environment (Deep Tech Europe, 2020).

The EU Innovation Fund (IF), established under the EU ETS for the period 2021-2030, will support the demonstration of low-carbon technologies and processes in energy-intensive industries, carbon capture and utilisation and storage of carbon dioxide, innovative renewable energy and energy storage technologies. The IF has been endowed with at least 450 million carbon allowances, with a value at carbon price levels at time of writing of about €11 billion. One approach to further scale-up the IF would be to rapidly reduce the number of allowances allocated for free under the ETS, and to use the resulting revenues for the IF.

The European Institute of Innovation and Technology (EIT) is an independent body created by the EU in 2008 to strengthen Europe's ability to innovate. The EIT is an integral part of the EU's Framework Programme for Research and Innovation. The Institute seeks to promote innovation across Europe by helping business, education and research organisations collaborate and work on pressing global challenges. In particular, the EIT supports the development of pan-European partnerships among companies, research labs and universities – so-called EIT Innovation Communities (Knowledge and Innovation Communities, KICs). Each KIC is dedicated to finding solutions to a specific global challenge. Of the eight KICs at time of writing, at least five are strongly relevant in the context of green industrial policy: EIT Climate-KIC: Innovation for climate action; EIT InnoEnergy; EIT Manufacturing; EIT Raw Materials; and EIT Urban Mobility. The additional KICs are: EIT Digital; EIT Food; and EIT Health.

7.3.5 Investment
Investment is a key part of a green industrial policy. The EU has at its disposal two main green investment vehicles: its budget

(the Multiannual Financial Framework, MFF) and the European Investment Bank (EIB).

The MFF covers spending areas from agriculture to cohesion, from research and innovation to environment, from single market to security and defence. EU leaders agreed in July 2020 to equip the EU with a budget of €1074.3 billion for the period 2021-2027. They also agreed on a post-COVID-19 recovery fund, known as Next Generation EU (NGEU), amounting to €750 billion for the period 2021-2024[18]. EU leaders agreed an overall target for 30 percent of the total amount of expenditure from the MFF and NGEU to be climate-related spending. Furthermore, the European Commission also requires each national post-COVID-19 recovery and resilience plan to dedicate a minimum of 37 percent to climate expenditure. Consequently, in different forms and with different timing, between 2021 and 2027 around €550 billion in 'fresh' EU resources will be made available for the green transition. This represents roughly a quarter of the estimated €300 billion per year required to reduce greenhouse gas emissions by 50 to 55 percent by 2030 compared to 1990. Given this order of magnitude, it is clear that only the private sector is in a position to deliver the necessary investment for the green transition. However, if properly invested, the EU funds have a major role to play, also by leveraging additional investment from governments and the private sector. This is particularly true for the so-called 'enabling investments', such as investing in smart electricity grids or electric-car charging infrastructure, which are necessary to unlock private-sector investment in clean energy and mobility

---

18 The European Commission will be able to borrow up to €750 billion on the markets. Capital raised on the financial markets will be repaid by 2058. The amounts available under NGEU will be mainly allocated to a Recovery and Resilience Facility of €672.5 billion (of which €360 billion will be distributed as loans and €312.5 billion as grants). Other resources will be top-ups of other MFF programmes, including ReactEU (€47.5 billion), Horizon Europe (€5 billion), InvestEU (€5.6 billion), rural development (€7.5 billion), the Just Transition Fund (€10 billion) and RescEU (€1.9 billion). Final sign-off of NGEU by EU leaders had not been completed at time of writing.

solutions. It should be noted that the 30 percent climate spending target should be handled carefully and could be overstated. Not all the expenditures considered to qualify for this target will truly be green investment, or even green spending, as a very diverse range of activities will be covered, ranging from agriculture subsidies to research and innovation funding. This likely overstatement is also a result of the lack of a clear methodology for accounting for climate-related expenditures, a point reiterated by the European Court of Auditors (2020). The development of a strong methodology and reporting system for monitoring climate spending is thus necessary to ensure that climate spending targets are translated into reality.

The EIB is the EU bank, and works, in cooperation with other EU institutions, to promote the development of the EU and to support EU policies within Europe and globally. In 2019, the EIB prioritised climate action, with the aim of becoming Europe's 'climate bank'. It adopted a new energy lending policy and sustainability strategy based on three pillars: i) end of financing for fossil fuel projects from the end of 2021; ii) future financing focused on clean energy innovation, energy efficiency and renewables; iii) €1 trillion of climate action and environmentally-sustainable investment up to 2030 (EIB, 2019). It should be noted that the volume of new lending disbursed by the EIB has declined every year since 2015, and its total amount of outstanding loans has fallen as well. The EIB has a margin of manoeuvre to act more forcefully: its capital ratio has gone up in recent years and its leverage has been dropping since 2012. Also, according to its statutes (Article 16.5), it can lend as much as two and a half times its level of subscribed capital (plus reserves and profits), which means its portfolio of loans could reach around €600 billion, compared to about €450 billion today (Claeys *et al*, 2019).

Monetary policy also has an important role in unleashing the financial capital required for green investments. There are various potential ways to do so, including focusing purchases of bonds on green bonds, applying less-stringent risk-mitigation measures to green assets used as collateral and imposing lower capital charges on green assets held by banks. European Central Bank (ECB) president Christine Lagarde has approved use of the ECB's large asset purchase scheme to pursue green objectives. She notably stated that the ECB *"has to look at all the business lines and the operations in which it is engaged in order to tackle climate change, because at the end of the day, money talks"* (*Financial Times*, 2020). In an important speech in July 2020, ECB board member Isabel Schnabel further developed this vision, identifying three major avenues through which the ECB, and central banks more generally, can contribute: i) through the ECB's involvement in defining rules and standards, and in promoting research for a better understanding of the implications of climate change for financial markets and monetary policy; ii) by ensuring that the ECB is itself an environmentally mindful and responsible investor, for instance when it comes to its pension fund investments and other non-monetary policy portfolios; iii) by taking climate considerations into account when designing and implementing monetary policy operations. These issues are at the centre of a vivid debate in monetary policy circles, with some taking the view that central banks must keep market neutrality as their benchmark in purchasing corporate bonds, and others taking the view that central banks should respond to market failures and take into account in their actions the risks that climate change poses to price stability. The outcome of this debate and any eventual decision taken in this field by the ECB will impact green investment significantly in Europe and beyond.

Finally, the EU can become a standard-setter in the green bond market. The global green, social and sustainability-related bond market reached €270 billion in 2019, though the segment remains a niche, representing about 5 percent of the total bond market. However, it is rapidly expanding. Between 2018 and 2019, it grew by 50 percent, and is expected to reach €338 billion in 2020. The EU is the biggest player in the market with 45 percent of global issuance in 2019, and the EU is where green bond issuance is increasing most, with a 74 percent jump between 2018 and 2019. According to a 2019 survey (Climate Bonds, 2019), 67 percent of respondents said there was a shortage of supply of green bonds. Moreover, respondents specified that regulation is the most effective way to scale-up the green bond market, with the development of a clear taxonomy of what counts as green being a key priority.

7.3.6 EU climate policy

All but one of the EU's member countries have endorsed the objective of EU-wide climate neutrality in 2050. This political commitment has not yet been translated into an operational strategy.

EU climate policy is based on a framework that includes bloc-wide targets and policy objectives for the period from 2021 to 2030. This framework, which also represents the EU contribution to the Paris Agreement, requires a 40 percent greenhouse gas emissions reduction target by 2030 (compared to 1990 levels), as along with renewable energy and energy efficiency targets.

However, the European Commission in September 2020 issued a plan to tighten the emissions reduction target to at least 55 percent by 2030 compared to 1990. The December 2020 European Council approved this target. The EU will now have to revise its climate and energy legislation to accommodate it.

One of the main EU policy tools is the emissions trading system (ETS), which covers emissions from the power sector, industry and intra-EU flights (overall amounting to about 40 percent of total EU emissions). Non-ETS sectors including transport, buildings and agriculture are dealt by the Effort Sharing Regulation (ESR, Regulation (EU) 2018/842), which requires EU countries to pay fines if they fail to reduce emissions by stated amounts.

Increasing the EU carbon price can be achieved by reducing the number of allowances put on the market by member states. This should result in increased revenues for EU countries because the price effect should largely exceed the volume effect. An increase in the carbon price from €25/metric tonne currently to around €50/tonne could be engineered by more rapidly tightening the cap, or number of allowances that can be issued to the market. Reform of the ETS is also increasingly seen as a way of raising resources so the EU can repay the €750 billion it will borrow for its coronavirus recovery fund (section 7.5). Reforming the ETS will involve major challenges including how to cut the number of carbon allowances given out for free (a concern for industry), how to deal with transport (inclusion in the ETS versus national taxation) and how to use ETS revenues (EU own resources versus national green investments and mitigation of the distributional effects of climate policy).

If Europe puts in place a stringent climate policy while other parts of the world do not, there is a risk that emissions-intensive companies might leave the EU with its high emission prices, and relocate to places with significantly lower or no emission prices. This is called leakage. This issue is set to become more relevant as the EU pursues a stricter climate policy, but it is hard to gauge exactly how significant an issue carbon leakage is. It has not represented a substantial issue for EU industry under the ETS (Claeys *et al*, 2019). Furthermore, the carbon price is one element among many others in an industrial strategy. Other considerations include energy prices, logistics, territorial legacy and innovation ecosystems.

In the ETS, carbon leakage is dealt with by giving emission allowances for free to companies in specific sectors. The allocation mechanism for free allowances is based on production benchmarks to ensure that companies have an incentive to reduce emissions but not to reduce production in the EU. But the granting of free allowances has led to massive windfall profits for some companies (they received allowances for free but included their nominal cost in the price of their products). It is not desirable to continue with this method to deal with carbon leakage.

The European Commission has said it will introduce an alternative system, a carbon border adjustment mechanism, with a proposal promised in 2021. A carbon border mechanism would have two aims: i) preventing carbon leakage by ensuring that all goods consumed in the EU, whether imported or produced domestically, are treated the same; ii) pushing other countries to also decarbonise. This would be achieved by putting a tax or tariff on the emissions embedded in imported products – or by requiring importers to buy ETS allowances based on what they know the exporters from third countries have emitted (Wolff, 2019). In addition, EU exporters might reclaim the cost of the emissions embedded in their products to ensure that European companies are not at a competitive disadvantage when selling abroad.

It should be noted that while introducing such a mechanism is possible, it would be a significant challenge for a number of reasons, including the technical design (for example, how to calculate the carbon content of imported goods) and the geopolitical repercussions, with some countries likely to perceive the measure as protectionist.

7.3.7 Single market rules: green public procurement
The new industrial strategy adopted by the European Commission in March 2020 rightly points to the fact that *"by providing a common regulatory space and scale, the single market is the driver of competitiveness and facilitates the integration of companies of all sizes in European and global value chains"* (European Commission, 2020a). The EU has two main tools to create the conditions for innovative, green, European companies to flourish in a receptive market.

The first, more general, tool is the completion of the EU single market. It is vital to develop a solid regulatory framework, focused on ensuring competition and access to a truly single market, with common or mutually-recognised environmental standards. Fragmentation in environmental standards, energy taxation and support measures for clean technologies prevent innovative European cleantech companies from scaling up in the way that their US and Chinese competitors do on their domestic markets. Coordination of national policies is key to avoid fragmentation of the EU single market:

"failing to coordinate would hamper the full exploitation of the size of the EU market and the related economies of scale" (Altomonte and Veugelers, 2019).

The second, more specific, tool is public procurement. In the EU, this is estimated to amount to about 16 percent of GDP (European Commission, 2018). Given its scale, public procurement represents a unique tool to foster innovation. For example, with the revised Clean Vehicles Directive ((EU) 2019/1161), the EU introduced national targets for public procurement of electric and low-emission buses and other vehicles. Such measures are important in boosting demand and promoting further deployment of low- and zero-emission vehicles. According to OpenTender data, in 2018 European countries procured transport equipment (including passenger cars, vans, buses and trains) for a total value of almost €19 billion. Assuming that most of this public procurement is devoted to motor vehicles, it is interesting to compare this figure with EU's electric car market, estimated in the same year at €13 billion[19]. This illustrates the order of magnitude of the role EU public procurement could play in creating a lead market for clean vehicles. Requiring clean mobility solutions in public procurement tenders can also support the transformation of the European automotive industry and could be a case of EU green industrial policy working.

Similar provisions could be introduced in the construction sector, which stands out as a sector in which European governments are important buyers, with about €100 billion in purchases per year. Such measures would contribute to the refurbishment and improvement of the building stock in the EU, which plays a central role in decarbonisation strategies, as the building sector is one of the largest energy

---

19 Based on European Automobile Manufacturers' Association data, we estimate that the value of motor vehicles registered in the EU in 2019 was €430 billion. Considering that only 3 percent of total car registrations in 2019 related to electric cars, we then estimate the value of the electric cars sold in the EU in 2019 to be in the order of magnitude of €13 billion.

consumers in Europe, responsible for more than one third of the EU's emissions. Furthermore, such measures could represent a major opportunity to create jobs and boost the construction sector, which is largely dominated by local businesses, while strengthening Europe's industrial competitiveness.

These two complementary tools – common environmental standards and green public procurement – can foster the emergence of the necessary ecosystem that will enable innovative green European companies to grow in a receptive single market.

7.3.8 Development policy

The EU produces less than 10 percent of global greenhouse gas emissions. This implies that to have an impact on global temperature levels, the EU needs to push its green objectives beyond its borders – also to achieve green industrial policy objectives. An important step in this direction was the European Commission's proposal in 2018 for a Neighbourhood, Development and International Cooperation Instrument (NDICI, COM (2018) 460). Starting in 2021, NDICI will bring together EU funding for its external policies in a single instrument. A quarter of the NDICI budget would be earmarked for climate action. With this tool the EU can increase its visibility and leverage in developing countries, notably in the promotion of green projects. Another important step would be to further consolidate and streamline EU development finance and climate activities outside Europe, which are today divided between the European Commission, the EIB, the European Bank for Reconstruction and Development and EU countries.

8 Conclusions and policy recommendations

As this Blueprint illustrates, green industrial policy is complex. For the European Union, we recommend development of a green industrial policy based on eight principles, as derived from the literature and case studies:

1. Strong governance
2. Tackling geographical fragmentation
3. Managing long-term expectations with a solid EU decarbonisation trajectory
4. Development of sound public-private partnerships
5. Stimulating EU green investment
6. Stimulating EU green science and innovation
7. A global approach
8. Transparent communication

8.1 Strong governance

Given the complexities of both green industrial policy and the EU as policy-making machinery, strong governance is a prerequisite for effective EU green industrial policy. It is crucial for efficient coordination of different types of stakeholders and for management of different policy governance areas, different instruments and different projects. First, the various partners must be incentivised with a set of balanced, clear, credible and time-consistent commitments. Second, it is necessary to set clear and realistic intermediate goals throughout the process to promote more risk taking. Third, flexible policy design is required to cope with the uncertainties of new green technologies, with clear intermediate targets and milestones that can be monitored in order to strengthen policy measures over time. Fourth, it is key to ensure accountability, with incentives and penalties where needed.

Implementing all this requires strong governance, which should be based on three principles: competence, ownership and political independence. This could be provided through a governance body that is politically independent but still fully accountable. This will not be straightforward to operationalise within the EU institutional environment.

A green industrial policy governance body should be accommodated within the structure of the European Commission. It should ultimately be answerable to the College of Commissioners, chaired by the Commission president. In particular, the Executive Vice President for the European Green Deal (currently Frans Timmermans, who is also responsible for the climate action portfolio) and the Internal Market Commissioner (which includes industrial policy; the current commissioner is Thierry Breton) should be closely connected to this GIP body. Other commissioners with policy tools that need to be activated for green industrial policy also need to be closely connected. These include the energy, transport, cohesion and reform, budget, trade, innovation and competition policy portfolios. Of these, the last two are perhaps the most potent instruments at EU level to leverage EU green industrial policy into private investment and national and regional public investment.

Ensuring the coordination and cooperation of multiple government players, each responsible for aspects of policy needed for green industrial policy, and ensuring that they will work together, requires a 'czar' or designated leader or figurehead. This person should be selected externally, based on their skills, appointed by, and responsible to, the Commission president, and given political independence and broad powers to coordinate and run dedicated green industrial policy instruments, such as Green Missions and IPCEIs. This czar would be able to select a dedicated EU green industrial policy unit and advisory board, with external experts from industry, academia and civil society. The czar leader should be given clear and realistic targets, and milestones, for which (s)he can be held accountable, and which also allow for risk-taking and failures.

The advantages of this approach include the ability to find new creative solutions, go outside formal channels, and an ability to involve multiple different players in big-issue decision-making. These advantages would suit very well the governance challenge presented by EU green industrial policy.

8.2 Tackling geographical fragmentation

European green industrial policies remain highly fragmented, with a vast number of initiatives being undertaken at EU, national and regional levels with little to no coordination. Significantly different green industrial policies in different countries could undermine the level playing field in Europe – and thereby fragment the EU single market. Thus strong EU coordination is needed. Strong coordination at EU level also is of paramount importance to benefit from synergies from various local policy initiatives. Fragmentation exists in local industrial policy initiatives to support green technologies, and in local climate-change policy initiatives related to, for example, environmental standards or energy taxation. A fragmented EU single market for clean technologies and markets holds back innovative European cleantech companies from scaling up in the way that their US and Chinese competitors do on their domestic markets. It is vital to develop a solid regulatory framework, ensuring access to a truly single, competitive EU market with common environmental standards. The current fragmentation ultimately hampers the full exploitation of the size of the EU market and the related economies of scale.

The EU level can tackle geographical fragmentation of green industrial policy in three ways: through state aid control, the European

Semester and the regional RIS3 smart specialisation programme.
The European Commission should regularly evaluate national and
regional green industrial policy initiatives, which will create the space
for coordination of the various ongoing policy initiatives. One way to
coordinate national and regional green industrial policies would be for
the EU to leverage the national reform programmes developed within
the European Semester and RIS3 regional specialisation programmes
(Altomonte and Veugelers, 2019). The broad EU green industrial
policy framework should become embedded in member state national
reform programmes and regional smart specialisation programmes.
The EU should replicate the successful experience of the governance of
state aid, under which member states retain responsibility for designing measures, but it is ultimately up to the European Commission to
have the final say on whether these measures can proceed.

8.3 Managing long-term expectations with a solid EU decarbonisation trajectory

Climate targets are an important green industrial policy tool, as they
give a clear direction to companies and investors in terms of the EU's
decarbonisation trajectory. Setting strong climate targets for tomorrow, if backed-up by legislation to effectively turn them into practice,
can have a major influence over the behaviour of the private sector
already today.

The EU's pledge to reach climate neutrality by 2050 and its target of
reducing emissions by at least 55 percent by 2030 compared to 1990
send a clear signal to market players about the irreversibility of the
EU's climate trajectory. But to be credible, these targets need to be
supported by detailed legislation. After the approval of the stricter 2030
climate target, the EU will have in 2021 to issue a wide range of new
climate and energy proposals for legislation that will align its tools with
the target. The emissions trading system (ETS), the effort sharing regulation (ESR) for non-ETS emissions and the energy taxation directive
will be reformed. Major challenges will include how to cut the number

of ETS allowances given out for free (a concern for industry), how to deal with transport (inclusion in the ETS versus national taxation), how to use ETS revenues (EU own resources versus national green investments and mitigation of the distributional effects of climate policy), and how to design a functional carbon border adjustment mechanism. EU legislation on renewable energy and energy efficiency will also need a substantial upgrade. EU 2030 targets for renewable energy and energy efficiency at time of writing (respectively, a 32 percent share of final energy consumption, and a 32.5 percent improvement against a baseline) will only deliver greenhouse gas emissions reductions of 45 percent by 2030. The EU must find ways for its countries to deliver on higher targets in the absence of nationally binding commitments, and for private investment to be really mobilised (one example is simplification of permitting procedures for renewables). Other important areas of EU legislation, including transport and agriculture, will have to be revised to push the decarbonisation of these sectors.

Delivery of this legislative framework will be critical for the development of a strong EU green industrial policy. It should be noted that the difference in time horizons between policy planning and political cycles makes achieving coherent and sustained green industrial policy efforts extremely challenging. In this sense, clear climate targets – particularly if enshrined into law – also protect green industrial policy from significant uncertainty.

8.4 Development of sound public-private partnerships

To develop a successful green industrial policy, the EU has to be embedded with the private sector. Public-private partnerships are not only about activating co-funding, but are also ways to access skills, knowledge and information. This requires a high degree of interaction between the public and private sectors, and collaboration should be iterative since the solutions are not assumed as known, but only as discoverable. The literature and case studies show that the design of public-private partnerships can take different forms. Deliberation councils, investment advisory councils, round tables, public-private venture funds and smart development banks are all examples of ways in which governments can make operational the principles described above.

Our recommendations on EU green industrial policy governance include a strong element of private embeddedness. In parallel, we recommend expanding the use of the European Alliances format, which has already been employed since 2017 for batteries and since 2020 for clean hydrogen. These Alliances are important public-private collaborations at EU level and should become key tools for EU green industrial policy. Important Projects of Common European Interest (IPCEI) are a core element of European Alliances. A further broader and deeper application of IPCEI should be considered, to make the best of this tool.

The principles for a new green industrial policy should serve as guidelines when selecting and governing new alliances. Alliances should focus on addressing mega-problems covering the whole value chains of all relevant clean markets, rather than solving more discrete problems. The Hydrogen Alliance is already broader than the quite narrow Battery Alliance. EU green industrial policy should also employ a balanced mix of alliances involving already-connected value chains that need to be scaled-up and very early-stage emerging value chains with still-to-be-connected stakeholders, even if the latter are higher risk choices that will result in higher failure rates.

To ensure a competitive environment in which innovation is stimulated in the new clean markets created and supported by the EU's green industrial policy, and to avoid rent seeking, the EU should use its competition policy toolbox, while ensuring that the competition policy arm of the Commission has sufficient dedicated expertise on clean technologies and markets.

8.5 Stimulating EU green investment

EU green investment will be important to realise the green transition, including by mobilising funds from the national budgets of EU countries and from the private sector. The EU decision to devote 30 percent of its budget for 2021-2027 to climate action is good news. But this goal should be handled carefully. First, it will be important to ensure that the remaining spending does not go against the green targets, requiring a mainstream green monitoring of the EU budget and of Next Generation EU funding. Second, with current EU accounting rules, there is a risk the climate-related spending will be overstated. Not all these expenditures can be considered green investment, or even green spending, as they are very diverse, ranging from agricultural subsidies to research and innovation funding. For all these reasons, the EU should develop a solid methodology for monitoring climate spending, and to report on it annually (Claeys and Tagliapietra, 2020). This will be important to ensure that the 30 percent target is realistically reflected in spending choices – and thus contributes to the scaling-up of the investment component of EU green industrial policy.

The EIB should be allowed to do more on climate action. The EIB currently benefits from very favourable rates for borrowing from capital markets and it would be a shame not to use this opportunity to finance worthwhile projects that can contribute to the fight against climate change. If EU countries are (unduly) worried about the EIB's rating, a capital increase should be carried out. The European Council of July 2020 invited the EIB Board of Governors to review exactly this issue. This represents an important opportunity to take a step towards making the EIB into Europe's true 'climate bank'. The EIB should also be supported in further developing its role as intermediary to address network and information imperfections, in order to become a true 'smart climate development bank'.

The European Central Bank can help unleash the finances required for the green transition by using its operations – such as its large asset purchase scheme – to pursue green objectives.

8.6 Stimulating EU green science and innovation

The EU needs to invest more in green innovation. It currently invests less in climate-related R&D than the United States and China. To truly develop a green industrial policy, the EU must leverage its public resources and toolkit to scale-up national and regional public resources that go into climate innovation, but especially private investment in climate innovation. The decision to earmark 35 percent of the Horizon Europe budget to climate innovation is welcome, but, as in the case of green budget spending, it will be necessary to ensure that the remaining 65 percent does not end up working against green targets.

It should be emphasised that fostering green innovation is not only about availability of public finance resources. It is also about allocating public finance to the best areas and projects, meaning those with the largest socio-economic and climate returns that could not have been reached without public support. In this respect, particular emphasis should be placed on high-risk, early stage technologies with potential for general-purpose breakthroughs. Green innovation requires a significant dose of risk-taking by public institutions, and an acceptance that there will be failures. New support models that provide numerous and still sizeable grants in a relatively non-bureaucratic way are crucial to unleash frontier ideas. Green industrial policymaking should avoid deploying money only to safe bets with only average returns. In this sense, a new green industrial policy should be a portfolio, with some initiatives within the portfolio failing along the way. A portfolio with no failures entails no risks. In the EU, this is the spirit of the European Innovation Council (EIC, section 7.3.4), and also of the well-established European Research Council (ERC). Although both programmes are applicant-driven and directed at supporting frontier science and ideas, without any targeted calls, many ERC and EIC bottom-up proposals address climate change challenges and should thus be seen as an integral part of green industrial policy.

Within Horizon Europe, new climate change missions should be considered beyond the current three (box 3 in chapter 7). The Horizon Europe missions should be a key component of EU green industrial policy toolbox because of their direct relevance, and also because they put into practise the new industrial policy vision of an institutionalised process of collaboration between institutions, the private sector and civil society. Each mission has a Mission Board of 15 high-level experts and an Assembly that brings together a larger number of experts from academia, industry, civil society, finance and end-users. This innovative and interactive model of policy design should be further developed. But the missions should also have clearer targets, incentives and milestones to promote more risk taking, to monitor and ensure commitment and to avoid rent seeking.

8.7 A global approach

Europe produces less than 10 percent of global greenhouse gas emissions. To really make a difference for the climate, the European Green Deal must go beyond Europe's borders. Europe should thus fill the current vacuum in global leadership, and initiate and build global partnerships with other countries.

In connection with developing countries, we recommend that Europe should leverage its external development policy and make it into a vehicle for global sustainability. In 2019, the Wieser Group (Council of the European Union, 2019) proposed to create a European Climate and Sustainable Development Bank to fix the current system of European multilateral finance, which is characterised by overlaps, gaps and inefficiencies. The Group outlined three options for creating a European Climate and Sustainable Development Bank: i) building on the European Bank for Reconstruction and Development and the external financing activities of the EIB; ii) creating a new, well-capitalised, institution with mixed ownership (including the European Commission, EIB, EBRD, EU countries and others); iii) creating it as an EIB subsidiary.

A European Climate and Sustainable Development Bank could indeed become an important tool for exporting the European Green Deal, and thus a key tool of EU green industrial policy. Such an approach would first help meet the EU's climate finance obligations and thus achieve the conditional emission-reduction commitments proposed by most developing countries under the Paris Agreement. Second, it would enable EU industry to enter new, rapidly growing markets, a win for EU green industrial policy. Third, it would help economic development in the EU's partner countries, providing an invaluable foreign policy dividend for the EU.

A second-best, and perhaps more realistic, solution would be to establish a one-stop-shop through which all EU (and eventually also national) funding for development is channelled or at least described in a consistent manner. It would be a platform to make it easier for third parties to access these European development funds, and to provide a clear overview about who is doing what in Europe in the field.

8.8 Communicate transparently

Green industrial policy, like any form of industrial policy, brings with it the risk of political capture, and all the risks that generally lie at the intersection of the public and the private sectors. Transparency is critical throughout the whole process of green industrial policy development, and should include roadmaps and clear government communication. A process of open policy dialogue on the part of the EU should ensure a high degree of accountability, which is critical to the success or failure of green industrial policy. Getting citizens on board through transparent communication will provide more involvement, legitimacy stability to green industrial policy initiatives.

References

Aghion, P., A. Dechezleprêtre, D. Hemous, R. Martin and J. van Reenen (2016) 'Carbon taxes, path dependency, and directed technical change: Evidence from the auto industry', *Journal of Political Economy*, 124(1): 1-51

Aghion, P., C. Hepburn, A. Teytelboym and D. Zenghelis (2014) 'Path dependence, innovation and the economics of climate change', *Policy Paper* 11/2014, Centre for Climate Change Economics and Policy, available at https://www.lse.ac.uk/granthaminstitute/publication/path-dependence-innovation-and-the-economics-of-climate-change/

Aghion, P., J. Boulanger and E. Cohen (2011) 'Rethinking industrial policy', *Policy Brief* 2011/04, *Bruegel*, available at https://www.bruegel.org/2011/06/rethinking-industrial-policy/

Aghion, P., J. Cai, M. Dewatripont, L. Du, A. Harrison and P. Legros (2015) 'Industrial policy and competition', *American Economic Journal: Macroeconomics* 7(4): 1-32

Aiginger, K. and D. Rodrik (2020) 'Rebirth of Industrial Policy and an Agenda for the Twenty-First Century', *Journal of Industry, Competition and Trade* 20: 189-207

Aldy, J. and R. Stavins (2011) 'The Promise and Problems of Pricing Carbon: Theory and Experience', *National Bureau of Economic Research*, Working Paper 17569

Altenburg T., C. Assmann, D. Rodrik, E. Padilla, S. Ambec, M. Esposito ... and S. Averous Monnery (2017) 'Green industrial policy: Concept, policies, country experiences', Report, UN Environment Programme, available at https://www.unenvironment.org/resources/report/green-industrial-policy-concept-policies-country-experiences

Altenburg T., O. Johnson and H. Schmitz (2015) 'Rent management – The Heart of Green Industrial Policy', *New Political Economy* 20(6): 812-831

Altenburg, T. and D. Rodrik (2017) 'Green industrial policy: Accelerating structural change towards wealthy green economies', *Green Industrial Policy*

Altomonte, C. and R. Veugelers (2019) 'Memo to the Commissioner responsible for Single Market and Industry', in M. Demertzis and G. Wolff (eds) Braver, greener, fairer: Memos to the EU leadership 2019-2024, *Bruegel*, available at https://bruegel.org/2019/09/memos-2019/

Ambroziak, A.A (2017) *The New Industrial Policy of the European Union*, Springer

Andreoni, A. and H.J. Chang (2019) 'The political economy of industrial policy: Structural interdependencies, policy alignment and conflict management', *Structural Change and Economic Dynamics* 48: 136-150

Baldwin, R. (1969) 'The Case against Infant-Industry Tariff Protection', *Journal of Political Economy* 77: 295-305

Barbieri, N., A. Marzucchi and U. Rizzo (2020) 'Knowledge sources and impacts on subsequent inventions: Do green technologies differ from non-green ones?' *Research Policy* 49(2): 103901

Bergamini, E. and G. Zachmann (2020) 'Understanding the European Union's regional potential in low-carbon technologies, *Working Paper* 07/2020, *Bruegel*

Bowles, S. and W. Carlin (2020) 'Shrinking capitalism', *American Economic Review, Papers and Proceedings* 110: 372-377

BMWi (2019) 'A Franco-German Manifesto for a European industrial policy fit for the 21st Century', Bundesministerium für Wirtschaft und Energie, available at https://www.bmwi.de/Redaktion/DE/Downloads/F/franco-german-manifesto-for-a-european-industrial-policy.pdf

Chang, H.J. (2019) 'Economics for People', Institute for the *New Economic Thinking*, available at https://www.ineteconomics.org/perspectives/videos/economics-for-people

Cherif, R. and F. Hasanov (2019) 'The Return of the Policy That Shall Not Be Named: Principles of Industrial Policy', *Working Paper* 19/74, International Monetary Fund

Claeys, G., S. Tagliapietra and G. Zachmann (2019) 'How to make the European Green Deal work?' *Policy Contribution* 2019/13, *Bruegel*, available at https://www.bruegel.org/wp-content/uploads/2019/11/PC-13_2019-151119.pdf

Claeys, G. and S. Tagliapietra (2020) 'Is the EU Council agreement aligned with the Green Deal ambitions?' *Bruegel* Blog, 23 July, available at https://www.bruegel.org/2020/07/is-the-eu-council-agreement-aligned-with-the-green-deal-ambitions/

Climate Bonds (2019) *Green Bond European Investor Survey 2019*, available at https://www.climatebonds.net/resources/reports/green-bond-european-investor-survey-2019

Coady D., I. Parry, N. Le and B. Shang (2019) 'Global Fossil Fuel Subsidies Remain Large: An Update Based on Country-Level Estimates', *Working Paper* 89, International Monetary Fund (IMF), available at https://www.imf.org/en/Publications/WP/Issues/2019/05/02/Global-Fossil-Fuel-Subsidies-Remain-Large-An-Update-Based-on-Country-Level-Estimates-46509

Cook, J. and C.Y.C. Lin Lawell (2020) 'Wind turbine shutdowns and upgrades in Denmark: Timing decisions and the impact of government policy', *The Energy Journal* 41(3)

Council of the European Union (2019) 'Europe in the world: The future of the European financial architecture for development', available at https://www.consilium.europa.eu/media/40967/efad-report_final.pdf

Deep Tech Europe (2020) European Innovation Council Pilot: Impact Report 2020, Publications Office of the European Union, Luxembourg, available at https://ec.europa.eu/research/eic/pdf/ec_rtd_eic-vision-roadmap-impact.pdf

Edenhofer O., K. Seyboth, F. Creutzig and S. Schlömer (2013) 'On the Sustainability of Renewable Energy Sources', *Annual Review of Environment and Resources* 38: 169-200

El-Shagi, M., C. Michelsen and S. Rosenschon (2014) 'Regulation, innovation and technology diffusion: Evidence from building energy efficiency standards in Germany', *DIW Berlin German Institute for Economic Research* Discussion Paper No. 1371

European Commission (2012) 'EU State Aid Modernisation (SAM)', COM (2012) 209

European Commission (2014) 'Criteria for the analysis of the compatibility with the internal market of State aid to promote the execution of important projects of common European interest', *Official journal of the European Union* 2014/C 188/02

European Commission (2018) 'A Clean Planet for all A European strategic long-term vision for a prosperous, modern, competitive and climate neutral economy, COM (2018) 773 final

European Commission (2019a) 'State aid: Commission approves €3.2 billion public support by seven Member States for a pan-European research and innovation project in all segments of the battery value chain', available at https://ec.europa.eu/commission/presscorner/detail/en/ip_19_6705

European Commission (2019b) 'Horizon Europe the next EU research and innovation investment programme (2021-2027)', available at https://ec.europa.eu/info/sites/info/files/research_and_innovation/strategy_on_research_and_innovation/presentations/horizon_europe_en_investing_to_shape_our_future.pdf

European Commission (2020a) 'Making Europe's business future-ready: A new Industrial Strategy for a global, competitive, green and digital Europe', available at https://ec.europa.eu/commission/presscorner/detail/en/IP_20_416

European Commission (2020b) 'European Battery alliance', available at https://ec.europa.eu/growth/industry/policy/european-battery-alliance_fi

European Commission (2020c) 'European Clean Hydrogen Alliance', available at https://ec.europa.eu/commission/presscorner/detail/en/FS_20_1297

European Commission (2020d) 'Enhanced European Innovation Council (EIC) pilot: investment opportunities', available at https://ec.europa.eu/research/eic/index.cfm?pg=investing#about

EIB (2019) 'EU Bank launches ambitious new climate strategy and Energy Lending Policy', European Investment Bank, available at https://www.eib.org/en/press/all/2019-313-eu-bank-launches-ambitious-new-climate-strategy-and-energy-lending-policy

Evans, P. (1995) *Embedded autonomy: States and industrial transformation*, Princeton University Press, Princeton

Fernández-Arias E., R. Hausmann, and U. Panizza (2020) 'Smart Development Banks', *Journal of Industry Competition and Trade* 20(2): 395-420

Financial Times (2020) 'Lagarde puts green policy top of agenda in ECB bond buying', July 8, available at https://www.ft.com/content/f776ea60-2b84-4b72-9765-2c084bff6e32

Foreman-Peck, J. (2006) 'Industrial policy in Europe in the 20th century', *EIB papers* 11(1): 36-62

Ghisetti, C., A. Marzucchi and S. Montresor (2015) 'The Open Eco-innovation Mode. An Empirical Investigation of Eleven European Countries' *Research Policy* 44(5): 1080-1093

Goldstein, A.P. and V. Narayanamurti (2018) 'Simultaneous Pursuit of Discovery and Invention in the US Department of Energy', *Research Policy* 47(8): 1505-1512

Gruber, H. (2017) 'Innovation, skills and investment: a digital industrial policy for Europe', *Economia e Politica Industriale* 44: 327-343

Hallegatte, S., M. Fay and A. Vogt-Schilb (2013) 'Green Industrial Policies: When and How', *Policy Research Working Paper* 6677, The World Bank, available at https://openknowledge.worldbank.org/handle/10986/16892

Hardin, G. (1968) 'The Tragedy of the Commons', *Science* 162(3859): 1243-1248

Haskel, J. and S. Westlake (2018) *Capitalism without capital*, Princeton University Press, Princeton

Hvelplund, F. (2005) *Handbook of renewable energies in the European Union*, Peter Lang, Frankfurt

Kemp, R. (2010) 'The Dutch energy transition approach', *International Economics and Economic Policy* 7: 291-316

Kemp, R. and B. Never (2017) 'Green transition, industrial policy, and economic development', *Oxford Review of Economic Policy* 33(1): 66-84

Klaassen, G., A. Miketa, K. Larsen and T. Sundqvist (2005) 'The impact of R&D on innovation for wind energy in Denmark, Germany and the United Kingdom', *Ecological Economics* 54(2-3): 227-240

Lane, N. (2019) 'Manufacturing revolutions: Industrial policy and industrialization in South Korea', *Working paper*, Institute for International Economic Studies

Lütkenhorst, W., T. Altenburg, A. Pegels and G. Vidican (2014) 'Green industrial policy: Managing transformation under uncertainty', *Discussion Paper* 28, Deutsches Institut für Entwicklungspolitik

Mazzucato, M. (2011) 'The entrepreneurial state', *Soundings* 49: 131-142

Mazzucato, M. (2018) *Mission-oriented research & innovation in the European Union*, Publications Office of the European Union, Luxembourg, available at https://op.europa.eu/en/publication-detail/-/publication/5b2811d1-16be-11e8-9253-01aa75ed71a1/language-en

Mazzucato, M. and C.C. Penna (2016) 'Beyond market failures: The market creating and shaping roles of state investment banks', *Journal of Economic Policy Reform* 19(4): 305-326

Mendonça, M. and S. Lacey (2009) 'Stability, participation and transparency in renewable energy policy: Lessons from Denmark and the United States', *Policy and Society* 27(4): 379-398

Noland, M. and H. Pack (2003) *Industrial Policy in an Era of Globalization: Lessons from Asia*, Peterson Institute for International Economics, Washington DC

Owen, G. (2012) 'Industrial policy in Europe since the Second World War: what has been learnt?' *Occasional Paper* 1/2012, European Centre for International Political Economy (ECIPE), available at https://ecipe.org/publications/industrial-policy-europe-second-world-war-what-has-been-learnt/

Paris Tech Review (2012) 'The German solar energy crisis: Looking for the right incentive scheme', available at http://www.paristechreview.com/2012/04/13/german-solar-crisis/

Rodrik, D. (2004) 'Industrial policy for the twenty-first century', *Discussion Paper* 4767, Centre for Economic Policy Research, available at https://cepr.org/active/publications/discussion_papers/dp.php?dpno=4767

Rodrik, D. (2014) 'Green industrial policy', *Oxford Review of Economic Policy* 30(3): 469-491

Rodrik, D. and C. Sabel (2019) 'Building a good jobs economy', *Working Paper*, Harvard University, available at https://drodrik.scholar.harvard.edu/publications/building-good-jobs-economy

Schwarz, L. (2020) 'Empowered but powerless? Reassessing the citizens' power dynamics of the German energy transition', *Energy Research and Social Science* 63: 101405

Stern, N. (2006) *The Economics of Climate Change: The Stern Review*, Cambridge University Press, Cambridge

Wolff, G. (2019) 'Demystifying carbon border adjustment for Europe's green deal', *Bruegel Blog*, 31 October, available at https://www.bruegel.org/2019/10/demystifying-carbon-border-adjustment-for-europes-green-deal/

www.ingramcontent.com/pod-product-compliance
Lightning Source LLC
LaVergne TN
LVHW061530070526
838199LV00010B/441